CITY ON A HILL

VOLUME 2

LIGHT OF THE WORLD

CITY ON A HILL

Also by Ted Neill

- Science Fiction -
City on a Hill
The Selah Branch
Reaper Moon

Snog Team Six Series
Volume 1: *Jamhuri, Njambi, & Fighting Zombies*
Volume 2: *Zombies, Frat Boys, Monster Flash Mobs*
Volume 3: *HALO Jumpers, Human Traffickers, & Tiger Zombies*
Volume 4: *Glam Rockers, Glitter Bombs, Murder Birds & Emo Gods*

- Fantasy -
Elk Riders Series
Volume 1: *In the Darkness Visible*
Volume 2: *Voyage of the Elawn*
Volume 3: *The Font of Jasmeen*
Volume 4: *Journey to Karrith*
Volume 5: *The Magus*

- Illustrated Kids Books -
Mystery Force Series
Volume 1: *Mystery Force Assemble*
Volume 2: *The Case of the Stolen Horn*
Volume 3: *Blazing Blizzards*
Volume 4: *The Case of the Peryton Thief*
Volume 5: *FRAMED!*

- Non-Fiction -
Two Years of Wonder
Finding St. Lo: A Memoir of War & Family
My Name is Ted & I'm a Racist

VOLUME II – LIGHT OF THE WORLD

Tenebray Press
© 2022 by Ted Neill
All Rights Reserved
Published 2022. Printed in the United States of America
ISBN: 9798362784249
Cover art provided by: Agata Broncel at Bukovero Designs

CITY ON A HILL
VOLUME 2
LIGHT OF THE WORLD

BY
TED NEILL

TENEBRAY PRESS
COPYRIGHT 2022

Genesis 18

King James Version (KJV)

[20] And the LORD said, Because the cry of Sodom and Gomorrah is great, and because their sin is very grievous; [21] I will go down now, and see whether they have done altogether according to the cry of it, which is come unto me; and if not, I will know. [22] And the men turned their faces from thence, and went toward Sodom: but Abraham stood yet before the LORD.

[23] And Abraham drew near, and said, Wilt thou also destroy the righteous with the wicked? [24] Peradventure there be fifty righteous within the city: wilt thou also destroy and not spare the place for the fifty righteous that are therein? [25] That be far from thee to do after this manner, to slay the righteous with the wicked: and that the righteous should be as the wicked, that be far from thee: Shall not the Judge of all the earth do right?

[26] And the LORD said, If I find in Sodom fifty righteous within the city, then I will spare all the place for their sakes.

[27] And Abraham answered and said, Behold now, I have taken upon me to speak unto the LORD, which am but dust and ashes: [28] Peradventure there shall lack five of the fifty righteous: wilt thou destroy all the city for lack of five? And he said, If I find there forty and five, I will not destroy it.

[29] And he spake unto him yet again, and said, Peradventure there shall be forty found there. And he said, I will not do it for forty's sake.

[30] And he said unto him, Oh let not the LORD be angry, and I will speak: Peradventure there shall thirty be found there. And he said, I will not do it, if I find thirty there.

[31] And he said, Behold now, I have taken upon me to speak unto the LORD: Peradventure there shall be twenty found there. And he said, I will not destroy it for twenty's sake.

[32] And he said, Oh let not the LORD be angry, and I will speak yet but this once: Peradventure ten shall be found there. And he said, I will not destroy it for ten's sake.

[33] And the LORD went his way, as soon as he had left communing with Abraham: and Abraham returned unto his place.

Chapter 10
Cell

Sabrina wished that Lindsey had shot her. Her life over, she would not have had to endure this humiliation, this betrayal. The other occultists stripped her of her weapons, her grapple, her visor, and after fumbling with it, the power pack on her belt that drove her patrol suit. Blindfolded, gagged, hands bound, she was led roughly down a hallway, the hands of strangers—*occultists*—under her armpits. Her captors interpreted her weaving, arrhythmic steps as resistance and shoved her harder. They were wrong. The pain from her knee, from Lindsey's deception … Sabrina could not walk a straight line. Lindsey's feeble protests, the sound of her voice, "Don't hurt her, she is my friend," simply made the weakness taking over her body worse.

Was she one of them, all this time?

Intermittently Sabrina's training surfaced. She tried to pick out voices, determine a sense of direction, but each time she found her sharpness elusive, pushed out of reach by her emotions, the tide of Lindsey's betrayal.

She heard a heavy door open. Someone called it a meat locker. They pushed her inside. The echoes felt close. She paced the sides. Before she made a full circuit, she vomited. She wretched until there was nothing left in her stomach, staggered across the room, slid down the wall to the floor. The back of her throat burned like an ember was lodged there. Her knees were hot and wet with the contents of her stomach. The locker was too small to escape from the foul odor. Nausea returned, irresistible. She vomited again.

Eventually she heard people outside, and the door opened. Lindsey's voice, cracking, as she took in the sight of Sabrina, slumped, covered in her own vomit. "Sabrina. Sabrina, I'm so sorry." Lindsey was immediately beside her, a warm hand on her cheek, in her hair. The blindfold was removed, and Lindsey's face was before her, tears dropping from her lashes. "I'm so sorry. I did not want you to find out this way."

She was wearing one of her ridiculous patchwork dresses that mixed floral patterns with skulls and crossbones. It stopped just at the knee, like a schoolgirl's. Over it was a cardigan she had also made, but with one sleeve red, the other blue and the rest green. The entire image blurred. Lindsey tried to wipe Sabrina's tears with the blindfold.

"Don't touch me."

Lindsey hesitated, then in a quick forceful gesture, wiped the vomit from Sabrina's nose, mouth, and chin before tossing the blindfold to the floor. The light changed as a figure moved in the doorway. Sabrina was vaguely aware that he held a rifle across his chest, but her eyes remained fixed on the stained knees of her trousers. An acidic, mashed-up mess of her lunch of olives and flatbread clung to the fabric.

"Please don't cry Sabrina. You never cry. You're the strong one."

"No, I'm not. Not anymore."

"Stop," Lindsey said, her voice firm. "Sabrina, you've been my strength when there was nothing else for me to turn to."

"For this? Why didn't you tell me?" On some unreasonable level, Sabrina was jealous, jealous that as Lindsey's best friend she was never let in on her secret life, that she was somehow not close enough to be told, to be trusted. Now all these people had a piece of Lindsey that she did not. What did that leave her with? She felt sick again.

"Sabrina," Lindsey said, her voice free of tears now. "Remember watching the sun set over the water in the summers? How we would climb up on the roof and the tiles would be so hot that they would burn our bottoms through our clothes." She paused, as if waiting for Sabrina to acknowledge the memory, but Sabrina would not give her the pleasure. She continued anyway. "Remember the smell of jasmine and watching the first stars appearing in the west, and the sense, the sense that there was something behind the beauty that we could not capture in words, something transcendent, universal, eternal even?"

"I remember," Sabrina said. "But it's not intangible. You can capture it in your paintings."

"Merely shadows, Sabrina."

"Not to me." Sabrina dropped her head.

"Please don't cry."

"Don't cry? But you left me."

"No, no, no. How could I tell you? I wanted to. All we share, but with D'Ag and your training, I couldn't burden you "

"So you betrayed me instead?"

Lindsey was silent.

The metal wall was cold and pressing against Sabrina's back. "How did you end up with them?"

"It was something in me. The sunsets were just the start. But even you can understand. Your sense of justice, it's innate in you, since the day you were born, but where does it come from? Beauty, justice, love, they all flow from the same source. We're all attracted to that source at some point."

It did not sound so terrible coming from Lindsey, and for a moment, Sabrina could see the reason in such *beliefs,* but then ruined eyes of the victims of the Cataclysm appeared in her mind, the whites burned out by a weapon with the power of a sun. A golden sun with six points on a wall in an abandoned house. A sword. A moon shaped like a blade. These were weapons of death. Not love.

"Then I found a flyer," Lindsey said. "It was all disintegrated and faded, but it literally blew up to my feet one day, as if it was meant to be there. I remember the words perfectly: *Is something missing from your life? Something more but you can't say what? Do you believe? Join the Underground.*

"It appealed to me. There is so much missing in my life. The beauty I can never quite capture in a painting. An explanation for my premonitions. Something told me I had to look. So I went out at night. Don't ask me how I knew they would meet at night, I just did. Maybe that was some sort of premonition. I'd sneak out, wandering into the Blocks, Stirner Street, Hills 34 and 33."

Sabrina could not help a protective shudder. Lindsey had wandered into places where she would not enter without a charged blaster on her hip. She was lucky not to have been caught as a scrit on the hills. And yet there was Lindsey, skipping along, the bells in her hair jingling.

"I know," Lindsey said reading the shock on her face. "It was crazy. I don't know how I didn't get killed, but I channeled you. Sometimes I'd talk to you, pretend you were with me. I'd walk like I'd seen you walk. When I had a close call one night and actually got chased by some men, I kept asking myself, 'What would Sabrina do?'" She knelt closer, her hand slipped down Sabrina's forearm, over her bindings, and closed around her fingers. "You were with me the entire time, you just didn't know." Their foreheads touched. "I'm so sorry, Sabrina."

For an instant, they were Sabrina and Lindsey again, but Sabrina knew this feeling of wholeness was not lasting. There was a crash outside, and the floor under them shook. The door groaned as it wobbled on its rusted hinges. The guard looked left then right, his eyes wide. Gunshots sounded from down the hall.

"We're under attack!" he cried.

A faint whine pierced the air and slowly metastasized. The cries of children. Thousands of children.

"No, no, no," Lindsey said jumping to her feet as she recognized the eerie sound of the L'ved's turbines. "What have you done, Sabrina?"

"They were going to find you eventually."

"Whore," the guard said, lowering the rifle at Sabrina's face and lining his eye up over the barrel.

The gun's retort cut short Lindsey's scream as she threw herself at the weapon. Sparks danced off the metal wall. The shot rang so loudly in Sabrina's ears she could not even hear the sounds of the scuffle as Lindsey held fast to the gun to prevent the guard from firing again. He was doing his best to try to wrench it away from her, prying her fingers the way a parent would pry a child's. With his other hand, he was trying to eject the cartridge. That was when Sabrina realized just what an old weapon it was. It was no more dangerous than a club until he rocked back the lever, removed the spent cartridge, and chambered a new round—an archaic bullet. This meant an opportunity to attack. Her hands were still bound, but she slid herself up the wall, stepped, pivoted, and kicked the back of the guard's knee. He dropped hard onto the floor, striking his head against the wall, but as he fell, his hand snapped the lever back and the old cartridge tinkled onto the floor.

He had a clear shot at Sabrina until Lindsey stepped directly in front of the weapon, touching it gently now and moving it to her heart.

"Marcus," she said. "The first bullet will have to be for me."

The floor shook again, and the lights in the hall flickered. Marcus straightened his finger out, away from the trigger.

"How could you betray us?" he asked.

"I'm not betraying you. I just don't want you to kill my friend. There is a difference."

The hallway was noisy with running feet. Occultists sprinted back and forth, some fleeing the danger, others seeking it out.

"What are you going to do?" Marcus asked.

"I'll stay with Sabrina."

He moved the gun to the side, placing the butt on the floor while he leaned on the wall to get up. His chest was heaving as he looked back and forth between Sabrina and Lindsey. He seemed to come to some decision before shaking his head and handing the weapon over to Lindsey. "You'll need this." He went to the door and limped away to the left.

The building shook again. Lindsey grabbed Sabrina and pulled her into the corridor. Sabrina followed Lindsey, her locks, braids, bows, and bells bouncing on her back as she ran the length of the corridor and down a flight of steps holding the gun by the stock.

Sabrina could tell that Lindsey knew this building well. They came to the main hall. People were pressing to the exits in a panic. The floor was a mess of overturned benches, twisted beach towels, and trampled pillows. Glass was falling out of windows, and dust was coming off rafters in sheets. A few occultists clustered in tight knots on their knees, their heads bowed while they prayed. Light flashed from the windows as if an electrical storm was overhead. Through a newly opened hole in a crumbling wall, the oblong head of an L'ved was briefly visible while it stalked through the adjacent section of the building, the hissing of its hydraulics and clumping of its feet terrifyingly close. A second flash lit the old factory like a bolt of lightning as the machine stunned fleeing occultists. A door in the same wall burst open. Unarmed occultists came running through in full retreat tripping over one another, their faces pale and sweat streaked. A second surge of armed occultists seeking to attack the machine collided with them. Women screamed. Children cried.

Another flash. Bodies fell to the ground. No one seemed to notice Sabrina. The armed occultists took up positions behind anything they could, benches, boxes, and tumbled walls while women and children retreated to a corner. With the sound of wrenching steel, the roof peeled back, and the jet roar of a second L'ved surged down upon them in a wave of heat and stifling exhaust. Sabrina and Lindsey doubled over coughing. On two blazing blue spears of fire, the L'ved lowered itself into their midst. Gunfire erupted all around them. Lindsey raised her rifle.

"Lindsey, no!" Sabrina cried and rammed her friend so that they fell to the ground. "Don't fight it."

"It will kill us all."

Sabrina thought back to what Sean had said and hoped it was true. "Not if you are with me. It will know me in my patrol suit." Her mind raced with possibilities. If they escaped, could they start over? She would look the other way this once. She'd do anything, just to get them both out alive. "Get me out of these cuffs."

Lindsey scrambled over fallen bricks to reach Sabrina's bound wrists. Meanwhile, the L'ved touched down, its talons flexing on the cracking floor. Projectiles banged noisily off its black carapace, marked with a white no. 7. A flash crackled from its fingertips, coalesced into an arc, danced among the occultists against the south wall, then traveled up a fallen rafter and dissipated. The fully struck occultists dropped to the floor. One man, partially shocked, tried to drag himself away on his arms, his legs stiff and paralyzed. They still had time, Sabrina thought. The L'ved was incapacitating but not killing. The machine turned to the east wall where half a dozen occultists were taking cover behind a boiler. Another bolt and they dropped to the floor like puppets with their strings cut.

Lindsey broke through Sabrina's cuffs with a craft knife she pulled from her pocket.

"Come on, we need to move," Sabrina said, scrambling to her feet. Lindsey led her behind a chunk of fallen roof as a third bolt felled a cluster of occultists running for the doorway. Sabrina brushed the residue of the crumbling ceiling off her suit.

It will have to know I'm here. It has to recognize me as a cadet.

Lindsey winced as she watched other occultists fall. A new wave of men rushed the room and began firing their ancient weapons while Sabrina searched for an exit. Stray shots struck the wall just over her head.

"Heyzoo!" Sabrina shouted, wishing she had not lost her blaster. A tall man broke from the crowd carrying a long rifle and charged the

L'ved. His eyes were wide with fury, his hair rising from his head like dark flames, his teeth bared.

"Into your weapons I send my ghost!" Anselem cried. Sabrina had not thought of him since the shock of discovering Lindsey, but he reemerged from the nameless occultists, a terrible reminder of the duty that had brought her there in the first place. His long legs carried him over the inert bodies of his comrades. The L'ved was momentarily turned to the corner, allowing Anselem to get within an arm's reach. He thrust the mouth of the weapon into the hydraulic stems and ribbed hoses that connected the machine's head to its thorax and fired.

The arc of white light ceased and the right arm of the L'ved splintered apart and reformed, a single serrated blade replaced the claw that had been there moments before. In one motion it split Anselem's rifle in half. In a second swipe, it sent his head flying from his shoulders.

"No," Sabrina said, the breath sucked out of her.

Before Anselem's body dropped to the floor, the L'ved's arm splintered again as armaments and panels rearranged themselves into a ring of spinning barrels. This was a projectile weapon as well, but it fired in such quick succession that its bangs were a sustained roar like a buzz saw. Lindsey screamed as the projectiles struck the occultists and their bodies were dismembered. Bits of clothing and flesh whipped into the air. Walls collapsed as bricks disintegrated into dust.

It was chaos. Those occultists who could, dropped their weapons and fled through one of the doorways to another section of the warehouse, but the first L'ved waited for them on the other side. The retreat reversed in Sabrina and Lindsey's direction and was soon overtaking them. Blood and burnt clothing landed all around as the

L'veds found their marks. *Fools,* Sabrina thought. All of them *fools,* for believing in the first place, now for resisting the nightmarish machines.

A fresh wave of occultists appeared in the very doorway Sabrina had hoped to escape through. They collided with the retreating mob and the momentum of both crowds choked. More occultists cried out, "Unto your weapons I send my ghost," before throwing themselves into the fire of the machine. Sabrina grabbed Lindsey and pushed her behind a fallen rafter. Blood, hot as water from a bath, fell on them as the occultists were cut down.

Lindsey's face was greenish and her eyes had taken on a stare of deep shock. Blood stained her clothes, hair, and skin. Her lips were moving, but Sabrina could tell she was sliding into incoherence. The hiss of hydraulics and the crunch of debris moved closer. A few more bold yells were cut short, replaced by the purring of the machine's servos and motors on the other side of the rafter.

The rafter screeched as it was twisted upwards and thrust away, and the implacable oblong face of the L'ved appeared, gazing at them through a cloud of dust. Blood ran down its obsidian surface as it bent closer to examine them. Lindsey screamed, crawling backwards before flipping over onto her hands and knees to scramble for cover. Sabrina threw herself on top of her, doing her best to expose herself and her suit. She did not know if the L'ved could see through the blood and dust, but green light lasered the clouds about them as the machine stepped closer. Sabrina wrestled to keep Lindsey beneath her.

"I am Cadet Sabryia!" she cried out, over and over. "Sabrina Sabryia!" A metal talon clutched her around her torso, crushing the air out of her and lifting her off the floor. Lindsey immediately began to run, but the other appendage reformed itself into a talon and closed around her. Her face turned red as she pushed and kicked at the machine. One of her shoes flew off as she continued to kick.

"Sabrina, help me!"

"She's in my custody! She's in my custody." The L'ved moved Lindsey closer to its face, green light dancing over the length of her body. *"She has surrendered!"*

A bolt of pain ran through Sabrina from wherever the talons touched her. All she could do was scream.

Chapter 11
Acre

Sabrina had long ago exceeded her allotment of hot water, but she still sat in the cold shower, staring at the drain. The blood, the dust, the ash were all gone. She was left with . . .

Nothing.

She barely felt the cold, although she could see her limbs beginning to shake, her skin taut with goose bumps. She realized the clicking noise she heard was the sound of her teeth chattering.

She wrapped her arms about her knees and pulled them closer to her chest and wept, her arms and thighs absorbing the sound of her sobbing. Leaving this stream was unimaginable. Here she could close her eyes and lose herself to the tumbling, tapping waterfall on her head. Under that icy drumming there was no past, no future, just now.

"Sabrina."

Sean was pounding on the door. He had been checking on her every few minutes. How long had he been pounding this time?

"Sabrina, say something or I am coming in."

"Go away."

The door handle shook then splintered apart as he kicked in the door. The curtain peeled back.

"*Iza,* Sabrina."

Her body was shaking as he pulled her up. She caught sight of herself in the mirror. Her skin had turned so pale that her veins stood out starkly, her lips were drained of any pink.

"I'm blue," she mumbled, shock taking over.

Sean's sleeve was wet and cold where he had reached in to pull her out. A female counseling officer appeared in the doorway. Sabrina could not take another stranger in her home.

"Get out, get out," she screamed. "Get *her* out!"

She struck at Sean, punching him, kicking him as best the small space would allow until he wrapped her in a large towel and then his arms, squeezing her until she could not breathe. There seemed a precise moment, when under the pressure of his embrace, her sorrow had nowhere to go and something inside her broke. She wept so violently and suddenly that she did not care if the other cadets and officers stationed outside her door heard.

She woke in her bed, wrapped tightly in blankets. The first thing she saw was the frame that held the picture of her with Lindsey's family at the beach. The photo was in the frame Lindsey had made for her. It exploded with color, its smooth sides broken by the ceramic caterpillars she had fashioned at the edges, each segment of their bodies a different color. The happy figures in the picture seemed to mock her.

When did it begin Lindsey?

Were you betraying us even then?

When could I have helped?

She remembered that day vividly. It was not their first trip to the shore, but it was the first time they had ventured out into the surf on wave boards. Timing her strokes to catch the momentum of a wave, riding its force, just teetering on the edge of chaos, did not captivate Lindsey the way it had Sabrina. Lindsey preferred swimming out beyond the breakers where they could float on their boards for untold stretches of time staring after the shafts of sunlight that continued into the sea's depths.

During one of these interludes, Sabrina had spied an unusual fish moving slowly below the surface. It was not until she pinched it between her fingers that she realized it was not a fish at all but a paisley ribbon gone loose from Lindsey's braids.

"You can do much more interesting things with your hair than I can," Sabrina had said.

"This rat's nest?" Lindsey replied, reaching up to her head.

"At least you add color and stuff to yours." Sabrina slapped the water with the stray ribbon. "Mine is just black."

"But it's beautifully black." Lindsey turned and re-balanced on her board. "Black like the sky between the stars. Black like the ocean depths."

"No one writes poems about the sky *between* the stars."

Lindsey's hands and feet slapped at the water as she moved closer. "But those things keep the sparkly, effervescent, and capricious parts in place."

Sabrina put down the picture before her tears blurred her vision. She remembered the day they had exchanged the frames, how she had felt a hollow open in her chest seeing the intricate artwork on Lindsey's: the suctioned feet of the caterpillars, the markings on their backs, the expressions on their faces. Her own was no more than a sleek, silver-black frame that she had bought from a shop on Searle Street. Yet Lindsey had hugged Sabrina's gift to her breast. When Sabrina had protested, insisting that she buy a more elaborate one, Lindsey had refused. "No, it's elegant, streamlined, tough." She ran her fingers over the steel of its frame. "It's you."

Sabrina rolled on her back and stared up at the ceiling. To her surprise, they had been gentle with her at the station, keeping the questioning session brief. But what reason did they have to doubt her? She had just brought in her best friend. Her commitment was unquestionable now. Not only that, she had raided a network of occultists on her own … well, not on her own, with the help of two L'veds. She had not been conscious, but the machine had lifted her out of the ruined building and deposited her at the barricades that the T-men had set up around the old factory after Sean had called for additional support. Since both machines had switched into a more lethal attack mode, it was lucky that she and Lindsey had been spared. The officers and T-men both were at a loss to explain it.

Her fingers traced the places on her body where the damnable thing had shocked her. Her skin was still tender, and her hands recoiled when she touched a particularly sore region. She slipped out of bed and crossed to her closet. Her communicator was off, but she did not bother to activate it. The noise of her footsteps roused Sean, who was sleeping, propped in the doorway, still in his patrol suit. One of her blankets was across his legs. His hair was sticking up from a night leaning against the wall. Dark circles ringed his eyes and he needed to shave. The female counseling officer had helped her to put on her pajamas the night before. She was by no means indecent, but Sean averted his eyes anyway.

"Hey," was all she could manage.

"Hey," he said, rubbing his neck and wincing. "I'm glad you slept."

"It had been a while," she said, pulling a dress uniform from a hanger. She noticed her patrol suit missing. She wondered if they would ever give her one again.

As if reading her thoughts, Sean said, "They're not going to enact any disciplinary action against you. You brought your friend in.

You led us all there. One hundred and ninety-eight occultists captured. People are talking about a commendation. No cadet has ever—"

"How many killed?"

"I don't—"

"Sean?"

"Fifty-six. At least that is the estimate."

She pulled the uniform off the hanger and stepped into the bathroom to change. It was no use trying to close the door. The frame had been shattered when he kicked it in.

"What do you think," she said, pulling on her trousers, "of a commendation?"

"As your supervisor?"

"As my friend."

"I would not want to be you." He seemed to regret his words immediately. "I'm sorry, I didn't mean—"

"I know what you mean," she said, speaking to her own reflection, a face she did not seem to recognize. "She's my best friend, Sean. Like a sister. If I had known, I wouldn't have—"

He silenced her with a *shush*, "I know. But don't say it. Not to me."

Strands of her hair stuck to the bottom of the sink. She pulled elastic from the nearest cabinet and wrestled her hair into a ponytail. When she emerged from the bathroom, she was the picture of a polished, professional officer. Sean straightened up and tried, without success, to flatten the hair on the side of his head.

"Help yourself to any food in the cold box," she said, picking up her comm-cube and clicking it on.

"Where are you going?"

The moment she activated it, the cube buzzed in her palm. There was only one message, but she knew exactly what it would say even before she read it. She could nearly hear the edge in D'Ag's voice as she read his words in the message field.

See me, immediately.

⬥

As she had anticipated, the guards and counselor outside her apartment door had received strict, if inexplicable, orders that Cadet Sabryia was to be allowed to move freely and unaccompanied as soon as she emerged from her apartment. Only Sean, who had been focused so intently on her, had not known. She did not offer him any explanation. Instead, she only waited to ensure that he would not follow her before she climbed into her CRP and started south for the Head Ministry.

It seemed as if her uncle's will had been enforced upon the breadth of the city. Traffic flowed in her favor, crosswalks remained empty. When she reached the Head Ministry, the front gate was opened and the guards remained in their control booths. She did not encounter a single soul as she marched through the halls. The heavy security door that lead to the most forbidden space in the entire land between the walls—the old city—opened automatically for her.

She stepped through into a different time.

The alleyways were narrow and snaking, the buildings alongside them a chaotic mix of shapes, sizes, and materials. Some were built purely of flat stones packed one atop one another. These were mostly collapsed, their interiors filling with drifts of sand. Other houses of hardier construction remained steadfast, the heavier mason-cut stones smooth to the touch and still standing in even rows. In some places, the walls were plain and utilitarian. In others, they were carved with alcoves for lamps, for shops, or simply for benches.

The alleyways were a maze with no plan or reason to them—nothing like the straight, eminently rational designs of Fortinbras and Lysander. Sabrina had always loved them for this very reason. It had taken her years as a child to learn them all but learn them she did, losing herself for hours, sometimes days at a time. She had never grown scared because she knew if lost, she could walk until she reached the ocean that bordered the old city on three sides. The Head Ministry building the fourth. It was when she had been lost that she had stumbled upon her most incredible finds: domed towers, soaring steeples, a courtyard of colonnades, gardens grown wild into a veritable forest within sandy, heat-cracked walls.

Now like old friends, the passageways offered her small details to help her find her way, a leaning column, a tree that had long ago broken out of its pot to spread its roots over the stone path, a rusting gate, a dry fountain, a stopped clock. In places she had to climb over the wreckage of wooden balconies whose rotted joists had sent them crashing into the walkway. In another she found her way blocked by a collapsed wall, noting the damage that time was taking with some sadness. How long before this magical place would be gone? But the ruined wall opened the way to the shore, allowing sunlight to flood into a passageway that had been locked in shadow for unknown centuries. Grasshoppers chirped and snapped into the air as she waded through the grass that had grown up between the collapsed bricks.

Along the shore, she stopped and listened to the gentle slurp of water slapping at the bases of the remaining buildings. Across the water, between her and the eastern shore of the bay, the ruins of an unnamed tower rode the waves, aprons of surf sloughing off its rocky base and swirling the long strands of algae clinging to its rocks.

How long would he wait?

She walked a few more steps along the shore before turning to follow the sequence of passages that led her to the tunnel that traversed the width of the peninsula. How she had feared it as a child, the long dark, unlit blackness. Now, in its tomb-like darkness she felt safe for the first time, completely invisible to the prying, judgmental eyes that awaited her outside.

If only my life could end right here, right now, in this darkness.

The wooden walkway beneath her feet creaked with each step as she progressed through the tunnel. As a child, this passage through the cold darkness beneath the city had always seemed to last an eternity. Now it was over too quickly, for she knew her uncle waited on the other side. Dim light appeared and the yellowing stones of the curving roof became visible again. A breeze pushed the smell of dust and mortar from her nose and replaced it with the scent of the salt sea.

Her eyes stung as she stepped back into the light. The sea opened up before her, the hills above Fortinbras, dim green outlines on the northern horizon.

D'Ag was standing in the sea.

The city had collapsed here where the waves had undermined the foundations of an old fort, leaving a crater in the peninsula. Green water lapped up onto the shelf, creating a large wading pool where the abrupt drop-off into deeper water was marked by piles of ruins that had once been the seaward buttresses of the fortress.

D'Ag was barefoot, his trousers rolled high to his knees, his ministry jacket replaced by a white shirt, its tails un-tucked and curling in the breeze. He would have been the picture of a relaxed beach walker if it were not for his stillness and his hands clasped behind his back so tightly that his knuckles were white.

So much for looking like a polished professional, she thought, removing her boots. She could not bring herself to roll her trousers. From the ankles up, she would cling to the appearance of an officer. *It may be the last time I can.*

He was standing beside a pile of rubble, staring into the deeper water. He did not move when she stepped up next to him. His eyes were red and the skin beneath them dark. She doubted he had slept all night. Sunlight, reflected from the badge on her breast, danced on the surface of the restless water.

"Here, some of the ancient invaders created a fortress," he said, his voice weak and soft. He spoke slowly, as if sedated or exhausted. "They were one host of many that invaded these lands. So many. All drunk on the certainty that what they were doing was condoned by a divine will. They killed for it. Killed, Sabrina. We are the only creatures that kill their own kind on such a scale. Why?"

A wave crashed between the piles of stone, its foam spreading out around their legs. His eyes followed the swirl of water as if the answer was hidden there. "Faith. Religiosity. Godliness. These things have caused more suffering, pain, and death than all the plagues combined."

He turned his gaze to the horizon where clouds rose up in ridges even higher than the green hills of Fortinbras—from this distance the metal fences and spires of lights and security sensors were invisible. Hills 36 and 34 were gentle slopes wrapped in blue.

"When they brought about the weapons that would lead to their ultimate destruction the scientists wrote that they had harnessed the fire of stars, the hand of the Lord, the power of God. They had seen His face they said. They were unlocking His mysteries for in unlocking the power of destruction, they felt that they had solved the mystery of creation. They thought they were gods themselves.

"Now this. This is what is left." He rested his right hand on the pile of stones, the crumbling brick covered in wild grasses, with barnacles and clams where the water swirled at their base. "These ruins were but a prelude to the annihilation that was to come. They couldn't see it, the warnings, the cycles of ignorance and violence. And so it led to this." He waved his hand towards the point where the sky met the sea. "A planet burned to a cinder." From some place deep in him, resurrecting his audio-comm voice, D'Ag added, "Religion is the disease and you … like me Sabrina … you have sworn an oath to eradicate it at all costs."

He turned to her, and her breath caught. Tears were streaming down his face. "I'm sorry Sabrina. I'm sorry that you now know the pain of that oath."

She swallowed hard. This was not the confrontation she had expected. Confusion melted into a strange urge to reconcile with him, even console him.

"The law is the point at which savagery ended because civilization stood in its path," she said, afraid she would not even get the words out. "You taught me that."

"Don't regurgitate at me, Sabrina. She was your friend."

"I had my duty."

"I am glad to hear that," he said. "But I know you love her and I do, too. I love her as I love you."

They were silent a long time, lost in the movement of water and wind.

"Thank you, Uncle."

"But I hate *them*," he said, suddenly bitter. "I hate them for their righteousness, their arrogance, their sanctimony. And I hate them most of all for dragging her and you into this."

"They did not seem violent or righteous," she said. "Not all of them. When I came upon them, they were peaceful. I think the word is pious."

"That is how it begins, Sabrina. It always leads to the same, blood spilt. Just as it did yesterday."

"I know."

"I wanted to protect you. I did not want you involved like this. I never wanted you to have to make such a choice."

"Did you know, D'Ag, about Lindsey?"

"I knew she was at risk. There were the warning signs: the creative, flighty nature, the charismatic personality. And of course there were the visions."

"But you continued to let us remain close."

"She was your best friend. I would not deny you that."

Sabrina noted the past tense.

"But I was always in touch with her parents, reminding them of the importance of adherence in regards to her medications."

Sabrina recalculated a lifetime of memories. She had never been aware of any contact between D'Ag and Lindsey's parents. It was no small thing to have the head minister call. Yet all these years, Lindsey's parents had never made mention of it, likely in an effort to provide a bubble or normalcy around their daughter and her orphaned friend. She wondered where Lindsey's parents were right now. Likely being interrogated in separate cells. Lindsey's brother Sam, too. But the thought of them was pushed away by a more unpleasant one: that she had so many times encouraged Lindsey not to take her medicine so that they could experiment with her visions.

"It's my fault," she blurted. "I've failed her."

"She failed you."

Sabrina's heart beat a little faster at the attack on her friend. "I can serve her and the city by ensuring that justice is done."

"On other cases," D'Ag said straightening. "You will understand now why you must be recused from this one."

Sabrina stammered, "But what if I want to speak on her behalf?"

D'Ag snapped his head around. "What? You can't be serious."

"For leniency in her punishment. Who better to speak up for her than the cadet who arrested her?"

"Sabrina," D'Ag said, his voice softened. "I want to see the right thing happen for Lindsey as much as you do."

"She needs help."

"Indeed, she does. You can stand by her as a friend, but not as a member of the officer corps."

Sabrina felt her face flush. She could hear her pulse beating in her ears.

"You already disobeyed me once, Sabrina. But nothing I could do could be worse than the punishment you are experiencing now. Don't squander the good will you have earned. You don't know it yet, but you are a hero. The commissioner has already contacted me to inform me that you will be receiving a prime commendation. No cadet has ever received such a distinction. It was not even my suggestion. It came up through the ranks. Stand by your friend, but as a friend. You have obligations to her but also to your profession."

She noted the strangeness of his defending her choice to be a cadet for once. A part of her could see the reason in his argument, but another part of her simply hated being told what to do as if she were a child. The wave of emotions she had been restraining the whole morning crested.

"What about this decision? Are you making this one as my uncle or head minister? And don't tell me it shouldn't matter, because it does. It does to me."

Her head spun with misdirected rage. She had lost and knew it by the look of pity on his face. She wanted to leave right then, but he answered softly, his eyes imploring. "I am asking you as the only father you have ever known."

The words, *How dare you* hung, held back only by her own flexing jaw. After a deep breath she turned. "Fine," she spat, "I needed some time off any way."

◊

Sabrina anticipated the stares when she reached the station, but not the nods, the handshakes, and claps on the back. The congratulations were restrained. Her fellow officers and cadets were sensitive to the fact she had brought in her best friend, but she had also broken up one of the largest underground occultist rings in history. The flood of discrimination that had borne down on her so long had reversed. It was so disorienting that she did not know how to react. The only officers who seemed unchanged in their distaste for her were Pitt and Boyle. While others rose to greet her as she passed them in the vehicle bay, Pitt and Boyle remained seated on the runner of a cruiser. Boyle occupied himself with a fleck of dirt on his visor while Pitt leaned forward to spit at the ground between his feet. To Sabrina, their normalcy was somehow comforting.

The two guards outside the doors of the detention wing saluted her. She returned them tentatively, willing herself to believe they were genuine. Xandes jumped up from her seat when she saw her.

"Cadet Sabryia, I've never seen our cells filled up so quickly. If you keep this up, we'll have to build another wing."

Sabrina had no response and moved quickly to her business. "I'm here to see Lindsey Mehdina."

"Of course," Xandes nodded, picking up a sedation stick and pressing an intercom button in one efficient motion. "Bring prisoner 7919 to Interrogation Room 2, please." When a voice answered in the affirmative, Xandes straightened so quickly that her white pony tail snapped in the air behind her head. "Please follow me, cadet."

As they made their way down the hall, Xandes offered her the sedation stick.

"No thanks," Sabrina said.

Xandes made a little "hmmph" sound, accompanied by a tick of her head. "Well, the guard will have one if she acts up."

"She won't."

The room was a bare rectangular box, the empty walls interrupted only by the mirrored window, banks of white glow strips on the ceiling, and a surveillance camera high in the corner. A red light switched on beneath the camera's eye indicating that someone—likely many people—were now watching as Sabrina settled into one of the chairs. As she sat down, she could not decide if her hands went in her lap or on top of the table. She moved them back and forth, uncertain.

The door opened before she was ready. It was the guard she saw first, a blocky man with a bald head, giving her a chance to let out her breath. Lindsey entered after him. She was in a white gown, the same as Jacob had worn. Her hands were chained to a waist belt that was linked to ankle braces. The metal jingled as she moved, a sad parody of her bells.

Her skin seemed green under the artificial light. Her hair bows were still intact, a scream of color that seemed incongruous in this joyless place. Likely they had not had time to remove them with the number of prisoners to process. Something about them reminded Sabrina of the way Jacob's tattoos had stood out so strangely when smothered by the white of the standard-issue prisoner gown.

Lindsey stared down at the table, avoiding Sabrina's eyes.

"Are you injured?" Sabrina asked, noticing the plasters on Lindsey's arm.

"Nothing serious. They patched me up."

"I'm glad."

A long silence passed in which Sabrina was acutely aware of the guard and the insistent red light under the camera.

"Have they told you what happens next?"

Lindsey swallowed. "I've been interrogated. They will process all of us, like they process scrits."

"Rehabilitation."

"Yes. Do you know what they do?"

"No, it's not part of my job."

Lindsey nodded and fell silent. Sabrina stared at the long empty table again. Would it always be like this between them now? Anything she wanted to say she stopped herself short. There were simply too many people, too many officers. And she was a hero now. What could she say that would not ruin that?

"Lindsey, I'm just struggling with why," she said.

"I told you in the locker."

"But I don't understand."

The chain clamored against the edge of the table and Lindsey slapped both palms down. Sabrina jumped. Lindsey's eyes were filling with tears. "You want to know why? Take a look at the picture of us with my family. You can see why in that."

A tear dropped into Sabrina's lap. "We were so happy then."

"Look again," Lindsey said. "You'll understand."

◊

A fresh patrol suit was waiting in Sabrina's locker as well as a new blaster. She put them in a carrying case that she dumped into the trunk of her CRP. Normally, she would have kept them in the front seat, but she could not bear the new reminders of her "duty" now. She rolled through the streets in silence, the stereo off, painfully aware that all the music stored in her roll pod had been selected by Lindsey.

She stopped at the intersection of Stirner and Comte streets, hating all the people crossing before her, walking down the sidewalks, or passing in their own vehicles. No one escaped her hate—not the market sellers, nor the bread deliverers, nor the cruiser officers, the teenage boys playing pitchball or the girls braiding one another's hair on a doorstep. They all were still living their lives, while hers had come apart.

She rolled through a few twisting old streets before she reached her apartment. It was still early in the afternoon, and the garage was empty. A cold wind blowing in from the sea struck her as she walked between support columns. As she pulled her uniform jacket close, she noticed a swirl of desert sand dancing across the garage floor. It reached the wall, and the wind animating it died, leaving it to fall, just dust on the floor.

The cold box in her kitchen was stocked with juices, fruits, and vegetables. Fresh bread and olive oil had been left on the counter. She thought of Sean and smiled. When she went to the washroom to relieve herself, the smell of fresh paint drew her attention to the repaired door frame. This was more than what Sean could have accomplished on his own. She realized the entire station was rallying to support her.

She wiped her eyes, glad to finally be alone.

Except that she wasn't. Lindsey and her family stared back at her from across the freshly made bed. She sat down on the mattress, the picture in her hands, her eyes moving over the people in the photo, then onto the caterpillars inching their way along the margins. She touched Lindsey, Sam, their parents. None of them had responded to the text message she had sent informing them that she had seen Lindsey and that she would be rehabilitated in a few days. No reply at all. But what was there to say to the friend who had betrayed and been betrayed?

Everyone looked happy in the picture. No hint of anything sinister. The figures in the background revealed nothing to her, neither did the clouds or the waves, the details of which she had already seen a thousand times. Although she tried, she could detect no coded message in the swirls of color on the segments of the caterpillars. She even rubbed each one with her thumb, waiting for some sign to appear in a smudge of paint.

Then she smashed it. She struck the bedside table repeatedly. The segmented bodies flew, their heads rolled, the frame itself left dents in the table, but she continued to pound it, the glass splintering and breaking then the frame itself until the backing snapped and the last intact piece disintegrated in her hand.

The picture fluttered out briefly before landing on the floor where the blue of the sky stood out in contrast to the white carpet. It was exposed like a precious artifact dropped from its case. Sabrina picked it up, her hand trembling, and turned it over.

Lindsey's writing flowed across the backside in looping pink letters. A single line. A single message:

Sabrina, find out what

happens to the scrits.

Chapter 12

Dead Lands

Sabrina intercepted the delivery boy outside the processing room. He was lanky almost to the point of gauntness, the sleeves of his jacket stopping well above his wrist. A few stray whiskers that had escaped his razor stood out prominently on his neck. Red bumps marred the skin he had successfully shaved. He smelled of self-consciousness, scents of acne lotion, cologne, and hair cream surrounding him like an aura.

"Excuse me, it is Daniel, right?" Sabrina said, shooting a glance over his shoulder to the double doors leading to the processing wing. "Can I speak to you a moment?"

"Sure," he said, rolling his chewing gum from one side of his mouth to the other. He paused to examine her. "That suit looks different from all the others."

"Newest version," Sabrina said. When she had put on her patrol suit that morning, she realized it was equipped with the latest enhancements—improvements Moshi, of course, had shown her months before. The newest gear usually went to officers first, not cadets. Clearly the station bosses had been searching for some way to show their appreciation for her actions in the factory.

She guided Daniel with a light touch of her hand around the corner so that they had a certain level of privacy. "I'm Cadet Sabryia."

His eyes grew wide and mouth opened so she could see his chewing gum drop from the roof of his mouth to his tongue. "You're the cadet who brought in all those occultists."

"That was me."

"Heyzoo, that was some serious stuff."

"Daniel, I'm not here to talk station business. I'm not supposed to talk about that stuff anyway."

"Oh, yeah sure, sorry."

She sighed. "Listen, my friend Xandes likes you."

"Xandes Phale?" He blew out a long sigh between his lips. *"Officer* Xandes Phale, the ice sculpture on the other side of those doors?"

"It's hard for her to show it. It's not easy being a female officer."

"She likes *me?* I think you have the wrong guy," he said, his thumb in his chest.

"You are the delivery boy—man that makes all the deliveries to the detention wing, right?"

"Yeah, but she never speaks to me much. Sometimes I say hello, and she just sort of grunts."

"She's got a terrible boss. It puts her in a bad mood. Listen, she just needs to know you are interested. Just show some persistence. I'll cover for you. I'll get you some time with her today."

"Why you doing this?"

"Cause she is my friend, and I'm tired of listening to her complain that she is not getting laid."

Daniel stopped chewing. He readjusted the package under his arm and lifted the bill of his cap. "Well, maybe I can ask her out."

"You definitely can, just remember, persistence," Sabrina said, slapping his shoulders and pushing him at the doors. He moved towards them with a deep swagger to his step and kicked them apart with his foot. He called out an enthusiastic "Good Morning" to Xandes. Sabrina saw the confused expression on the female officer's face before the doors swung closed.

She pressed her forehead against the wall. The patrol suit, using a helpful female voice in her ear piece, informed her that her pulse and heart rates were elevated. It suggested ways to lower her blood pressure when not on duty: exercise, reducing her sodium intake, breathing and stretching exercises. She cut the message off and tried to still her shaking hands. She decided the show of nerves might actually help her in the fraud she was about to perpetrate. When enough time had passed, she entered the doors herself.

Daniel's body was leaning at an angle against Xandes' desk, his weight balanced on his elbow. His hips were cocked to the side, and his other hand hooked on his belt.

"Cadet Sabryia," Xandes said, jumping to her feet and looking past Daniel. "How can I help you?"

"I need to see Durp. I can't wait in line," she said walking around the desk. "I'll take this for you." She swept Daniel's delivery tablet from the counter and headed for Durp's closed office door. She did not knock but instead slapped it open, then slammed it after her.

Durp's office was illuminated by the two dozen screens on his desk. Tilted towards him, they bathed him in a blue glow that gave his skin a sickly pallor. His hand cupped a greasy headset to his ear as he listened to the different interrogation displayed on each screen. His rheumy eyes, the flesh beneath them sagging, shifted towards Sabrina without a hint of surprise.

"Well, Princess Sabryia, you're keeping us busy down here," he said.

She made a long conspicuous scan of the room, noting the dirty table, the cold cube humming in the corner, and his jacket hanging on the clothes tree beside the door. The desk was covered with empty food containers. The reclamation bin in the corner was already overflowing with bottles, wrappers, and empty plates. She suspected it was the leftovers of a pitchball watching party. But she was most interested in the jacket.

"You sure know how to make a space feel like home," she said.

"They send you to clean it?"

She took a deep breath, clenching and unclenching her jaw while waving the signature tablet. "I'm here for the delivery boy. Apparently he thinks you are a sack of filth and would rather try to score a date with Xandes than speak to you."

Laughter erupted from him and he leaned back in his chair. "It would be good to get her married off. Loosen her up." His laugh subsided, and he patted his knee. "You got yourself a man cadet, or have you been too busy playing scissor sister with your friend down the hall?"

Her head felt light with a sudden rush of blood. "The delivery boy was wrong. You are not a sack of filth. You're a pile of fetid excrement." She sent the tablet spinning at his face. He snatched it out of the air, his hand seizing it like a clamp.

"Tell the delivery boy good luck," he said removing a stylus from the side of the tablet and scrawling his signature across the screen. It seemed strange to her that a creature like Durp knew how to write.

"I'll tell him to hurry up. His lorry is blocking my cruiser."

"As long as it's not blocking my sickness-seater. I've got a load of dead heads to ship to Dr. Horwitz." He held out the tablet. She crossed the room and reached for it, maintaining as great a distance from him as she could. Once she had the tablet in hand, he let his hands fall to his thighs. His lips smacked as if he was trying to suck a piece of food from his teeth. When she stepped back, the corners of his mouth ticked downward.

"New suit," he said. "Fits you well."

Sabrina felt the need to fill the silence that followed as he stared at her. "This office is a disgrace."

"It looks better with the lights off, like a lot of things."

She cleared her throat, glancing at the bank of screens. To her relief, she did not see Lindsey in any of the frames. She made a short path to the door.

"Maybe I should be more careful about what I say," Durp said. "After all, you *did* bring in your best friend."

It was the opening she had been waiting for. She turned on him, swinging out her arm, grabbing the clothes tree, and slamming it to the floor, the oversized jacket ballooning then deflating on the floor. The entire gesture elicited a "Whoop!" from Durp.

"You listen to me, you pus sucker—"

"No, you listen to me," Durp said through his howls of laughter. "You are going to have to clean that up now!" His guffaws mutated into high-pitched titters broken by wheezes. His cheeks shook and the skin on his neck turned red. He pounded his thigh with his fist. Sabrina swept up the jacket and tree in one exasperated motion and went to the door.

"Not that anyone would notice in this sty," she grumbled.

He laughed again, cheerfully, his voice echoing into the hallway. "You are all right, Cadet. You come back here anytime." He spoke as if they were best friends. In a strange way, she wondered if they now were, the insult being Durp's language of camaraderie.

Daniel was still at the desk, now turned so that both elbows balanced on the counter. He was working on making arrangements in three weeks' time.

"I'm not available that evening," Xandes was saying. "That is my continuing education night."

"I thought you said you had continuing education on second days," Daniel said. He had removed his hat and was scratching his head.

Sabrina passed them and flung the tablet at Daniel. It clattered across the counter, and he lost his hat diving for it.

"Cadet Sabryia, are you alright?" Xandes said, running from behind the desk to follow in Sabrina's wake.

"Durp is a pig."

Xandes looked at Sabrina, her eyes knowing and sympathetic at the same time. "Is there anything else I can do for you? Would you like to visit your friend this morning?"

"She's not my friend," Sabrina said, slapping open the double doors in a final, grandiose display of fury, calculating her outrage carefully. She swept down the hall, her boots echoing loudly as she walked in what she hoped was a pace that conveyed disgust, exasperation, and hostility. Two fellow cadets came around the corner and swerved to avoid her. An officer offered an enthusiastic salute, which she returned with indifference. The spectacle worked. By the time she neared the vehicle bay, she felt protected by a shell of anger. She did her best to maintain the air, even as her heart fluttered in her chest and her palms sweated as she clutched the access pass she had stolen from Durp's jacket. She checked out a power cycle and two extra batteries, loading them into the stowage cases on either side of the rear tire. She was not officially on duty, but in her patrol suit with her newfound reputation, no one questioned her. Administrative officers responded to her requests with swift efficiency. Haddon Blanchard, the head mechanic, provided her with the newest cycle. He was a quiet man with a reputation for being able to fix anything. He also boxed at the station gym and was one of the few people who would cheer for Sabrina when she was fighting an opponent. She suspected he would have ordered her the newest cycle anyway, but the speed with which his maintenance crew fetched the cycle, wiped it down, then rushed to open the rolling gate was novel. Haddon watched his men a moment, a half smile at the corner of his lips while he shook his head.

"How does it feel to be a hero?" he asked.

"Honestly?"

He nodded.

"I hate it."

Haddon smiled then began walking back to his office. "You have a safe ride, Cadet."

Outside on Avalos Street, she was relieved to be away from the station and able to act like just another cadet. As she set her cycle on its kickstand across from the detention wing of the station, passing residents treated her with the same wary indifference they would any member of the Security Ministry.

She waited as inconspicuously as possible, her visor down and hair tucked beneath her helmet, making herself as unrecognizable as possible. When a cruiser rolled by, she did her best to appear engaged with a palm tablet, tipping her face up and nodding to her passing peers only at the last minute.

In truth, the tablet was blank. All she saw before her eyes were the pink scrawling words:

Sabrina, find out what happens to the scrits.

Had that message always been there? Had Lindsey always known this would happen? She tried to piece things together, but the gaps were too large. All that was left to do was to follow her friend's imperative. Then maybe she would understand.

An admin officer from the detention wing walked out into the flow of CRPs and raised his hands to stop the traffic. A large door rolled open behind him, and the mirrored windscreen of the prisoner transport rocked into the sunlight. Distorted reflections of the buildings and traffic scrolled across the glass. The long, white double-decker vehicle barely cleared the bay doors. Its chassis sat high up from the road surface, lifted by all-terrain tires. Rows of tinted windows ran its length allowing some light in the back for the prisoners, but the windows were set too high for occupants chained to the benches to see through. Rolling along the road without being able to see out the windows made many of the passengers motion sick, earning the transports their nickname: sickness-seaters. Unlucky cadets were often given the task of hosing out the insides after the transport had made a run, and no amount of cleanser and water could ever eliminate the smell of vomit. Sabrina knew D'Ag would have objected to such an uncomfortable ride for prisoners, but even she knew a sick prisoner was a much more cooperative one.

A high-pitched squeal echoed off the buildings as the transport braked at the corner, CRPs moving past its bulk like small pups. The admin officer was disappearing down the ramp, the bay door closing behind him. The gears of the transport clanged as it began to roll forward again to turn the corner. Sabrina charged her cycle, pulled out into traffic, and followed.

◈

The carrier headed out along the coastal road, tracing a path around the foot of Hill 36. The road turned north, the sea opening up on Sabrina's right, wide and blue. She passed a few roll pod repair shops and fishing hamlets before the distances between residential buildings grew. Manmade structures eventually gave way to wild fennel and the occasional tamarisk tree, but even these were sparse. For the most part the land was empty. Empty sea and empty desert rolling past.

The traffic was light at this time of mid-morning. It was easy to follow the big white transport in such a landscape. The challenge was to avoid attracting the driver's attention. She held back behind a fruit lorry for a while, a dishcloth displaying the colors of the driver's favorite pitchball team snapping from the rear gate. The lorry provided her cover until a farmer, hauling a tractor, pulled onto the road ahead, slowing them. The transport shrank to a small white rectangle on the horizon. Sabrina kicked the cycle into overdrive, the wind rising around her, the machine's vibrations settling into a gentle hum as she passed both vehicles and approached a speed closer to what the cycle's makers had intended.

The sun was near its zenith when the transport slowed and turned off the main highway, heading west. Hills closed on either side and quickly concealed the vehicle, but the dust cloud left in its wake betrayed its path. Sabrina changed the terrain settings on the suspension and rode onto the dirt road. After a few minutes, the dirt gave way to jagged, pockmarked slabs, all that was left of an older road, likely built before the Transition.

They were in the Dead Lands. Sabrina had heard of them, but had never visited. These were areas of arid hardpan bordering the irradiated wastes that surrounded the former capital city. The wastes were nothing but radioactive ruins: fields of rubble and smoky glass where the heat of explosions in the capital had transformed the desert sands. The Dead Lands ringed the waste, a buffer, with pockets of radiation still high enough to kill.

Sabrina cycled through menus on her visor and placed a radiation monitor in the corner of her vision. The levels were elevated, but she was safe for now.

She followed the transport well into the afternoon. The air was hot and stifling in the hills. The planet's temperatures had risen after the Cataclysm, and here among the hills there was no sea breeze to abate the sun's power. She passed old orchards on either side, the dead stumps filling the fields like tombstones in a graveyard. Trees and shrubs that had held together hillsides had shriveled in the changed climate, their roots withering so much so that even the mountain faces decayed, their faces sliding off in avalanches leaving piles of scree across the road.

The carrier braked before making another turn. Farther up the next valley, she spotted an abandoned settlement on a hilltop, the houses still distinguishable among overgrown trees—the only green she had seen in hours. She charged the engine and climbed the road towards the houses. From the hilltop she could see the transport's destination: another cluster of buildings at the terminus of the road. The compound was surrounded by glittering razor wire fences. Green fields and orchards carpeted the land within, a stark contrast to the surrounding sea of brown. Three bulbous water towers looming over the compound were surpassed in height only by the comm-tower, one of the largest Sabrina had ever seen.

Sabrina kept an eye on the transport and its approach to the compound as she climbed the hill towards the abandoned settlement. The hilltop settlement was sealed by a crooked gate and a rusting fence. Sabrina dismounted in front of the gate and cut through using a set of pliers from the cycle's tool kit. She rolled the cycle forward and hid it in a narrow alley between two stucco white houses. She ran just below the ridge line, careful not to silhouette herself against the sky and found a vantage point to zoom in on the compound with her visor.

Two armed guards exited the gatehouse as the transport approached. One guard conversed with the driver while another walked the length of the vehicle. Once the inspection was complete, they waved the driver through. The transport pulled up to a building that was fenced, even within the compound. Detention guards, their white padded uniforms and sedation sticks recognizable to Sabrina even at a distance, opened the doors and led the prisoners out. The prisoners from the top row of the carrier emerged in an orderly single file, dazed, stumbling, and clinging to one another. The guards led them with little fanfare through a door on the side of the building.

The extraction of the prisoners from the lower deck was completely different. Sabrina noticed that although parked, the carrier was rocking. Additional detention guards came running into the lot and surrounded it, positioning themselves around the back door, their sedation sticks lowered. Three significantly larger guards held modified sticks with collars at the ends. After a pause, the guards threw open the doors and the prisoners came flooding out in a panic. A few guards herded them to a far end of the lot. They came obediently, running with their chains in hand. Sabrina zoomed in further, so close she could see the fear in their eyes. Those who had their wits about them, who appeared to be ordinary occultists, guided the scrits who tripped and scrambled about, confused and terrified, their memories impaired. Meanwhile, the larger guards with the modified sedation sticks rushed the carrier. More rocking. One guard tumbled out of the back door, a red gash across his forehead. Another jumped in to take his place. Eventually, the rocking of the vehicle subsided. The guards appeared at the back door with what appeared to be a single prisoner, a woman. Despite being in a collar, she was fighting, but her resistance went far beyond that of an ordinary prisoner. She moved more like a wild animal, bucking, swiping, and kicking, her gray hair down over her face as she threw her captors back and forth with unbelievable strength. Her hands were covered in blood, and when one of the guards pulled back on her mane of hair, revealing her face, her mouth was mottled in bright red gore.

The other prisoners were shrinking back in their corner of the lot as the wild woman was led through a different door. Four men had to lean on the two sedation sticks locked to her collar to force her through. An overwhelming sense of dread rose up within Sabrina. Her visor felt as if it would slip off her face from her perspiration. She reached for her canteen and swallowed hard, afraid that she was becoming dehydrated.

Water spilled from the canteen as she tried to replace the cap, her entire body trembling. She reminded herself it had been many hours since she had eaten and that she should have something soon.

Once the wild woman was gone other guards led the prisoners into the building. The lot was empty until two more staff members arrived. They stepped into the back of the vehicle and emerged carrying the body of a prisoner in a monomer sheet. Even at this distance, the stains of blood on the body were visible through the sheet. The hands hung out of the end of the sheet, the chains fastened pointlessly to the wrists.

The driver finally returned, moved the carrier to another lot, and carried a hose into the back to clean. When he was done, he shut the back doors and also disappeared inside the building, leaving Sabrina with nothing to watch but the empty lot, shimmering in the heat. She absently chewed some biscuits she had packed in the pocket of her suit, although she did not taste them. All her thoughts were focused on the image of the woman's face as she howled with animal-like rage.

After eating something, Sabrina was able to focus enough to watch for another two hours. The perimeter guards' intervals were of particular interest to her—they made a circuit every 30 minutes—and when the sun had shifted and afternoon shadows appeared, Sabrina was able to get an infrared reading on the watch towers. She was pleased to see no heat signature whatsoever—they were not manned. Instead, the passing guards used them only to gain a vantage point over the surrounding landscape.

In the evening, there was a great deal of movement between the main buildings of the central compound and the barracks in the rear. A squat building set in the far southwest corner appeared to be a canteen and the destination for a number of off-duty staff. It was likely the only place of recreation. The staff ate at tables under shady trellises, and smoke rose from a chimney in the back. The perimeter guards slowed and greeted their acquaintances when they passed.

Sabrina knew it was where she would enter the compound.

Chapter 13
5625

Sabrina dreamed again of the pink room and the painting of the sailboat, the white sail riding on the silver sea. If only she could turn, she was certain she would see what else was in the room. But no matter how her neck muscles strained, paralysis gripped her. Her eyes remained fixed on that picture until it melted away, the walls dissolving to a vision of the old city. Here the ancient residents were still living, adorned in their robes, belts, and shimmering trinkets. Melodious voices floated from the towers overhead, incense burned in shadowy alcoves, candles flickered in amber lamps. A bell tolled. Laughing, visiting, trading, *worshiping,* continued, the people oblivious to the ruin in wait for their coming generations: a scorched planet, a land of dust, a tomb of stone.

A silver orb floating in metal darkness.

A mother who has no mercy.

A shrill beeping woke her. She sat up panting as if she had been running, her hand instinctively on her blaster. When she caught her breath, she turned off the alarm on her visor and reached for her provision bag. It was nestled between the roots of a cypress tree where she had wedged it to use as a pillow. Her cycle was parked alongside her to block the wind, the white wall of one of the abandoned settlement houses doing the same on her other side. It was an hour before sunrise, and the desert temperatures had plummeted. She wrapped herself in her uniform jacket before eating a breakfast of flat bread and preserves. She stared into the darkness of the nearest house while she chewed. The closest room was just a shell, the roof blown away by a bomb. Round craters the size of her fist scarred the walls where bullets had struck. The remaining parts of the house were intact, but she had no desire to enter. Even when darkness had fallen the night before, she preferred to remain outside—the whispering sound of the breeze in the pine branches was infinitely more soothing than what desiccated human remains might lie inside the buildings. Outside, with a spray of stars dimming overhead and a few sporadic bird chirps, she could forget the carnage from the war and understand the allure of this homestead perched amid orchards, where the laughter of children had once echoed between walls and bougainvillea waved in the breeze.

But the children had been murdered, too, along with so many others.

She closed her bag and replaced it under the seat of the cycle. She used her natural vision to find her way back to the ridge. When she put her hand on a scorpion that had nestled itself into the nook of a rock, she pulled down the visor to use her night vision. Its stinger had not pierced her glove, but the species was small and likely fatal. She crushed it under her boot.

She crossed the spine of the ridge on her stomach, pulling herself along on her elbows, this time after a careful inspection of the ground for more scorpions. Once far enough down the hill, she took to her feet again, switching layers of readouts on her visor to study the fences in emerald night vision as well as infrared. Guards were up and moving; so were a number of figures within the buildings. Her sensors could only penetrate the first one or two layers of walls, but it was enough to tell that the early risers were starting their shifts.

Before the morning light could betray her, she rushed down the ridge, dodging and weaving between boulders and stumps that she had picked out the day before for cover. To her surprise, the new suit helped to steady her, its gyros and reinforced mesh responding, flexing, and contracting at various points around her body as she moved, keeping her from tumbling over when she began to lose her footing.

As she dived headfirst into a gully alongside the fence, she made a mental note to kiss Moshi the next time she saw him. The suit anticipated her movements, supporting her body as she curled and rolled for cover. The fence was twice, almost three times as high here, compared to the entrance. Cutting it would set off alarms. So with silent plea to Moshi that his ingenuity would continue to serve her, she jammed her feet into the gully face, took two steps, and jumped.

The servos and flexors hummed as they powered to full strength. She focused on building enough torque to turn her body and move her center of gravity. The suit responded, and she rotated, stretched out, recumbent on the air at the peak of her leap, then descended on the other side. She caught herself in a summersault and rolled into a crouch. No sirens. No alarms.

Two kisses for Moshi then.

The canteen was her next target and with the darkness lifting she wasted no time running behind it to a row of outdoor toilets. They were locked for the night, but one of the handles broke off easily and she stepped inside.

The strong chemicals used to keep the toilet sanitary made her dizzy. Her headset allowed her to eavesdrop on noises outside and within the main building. Doors opened and closed, footsteps crunched over gravel, a few terse good mornings, but still no alarms, no alerts regarding a trespasser, just the running water of showers, the clink of plates in the dish room, and what sounded like a member of kitchen staff speaking to another member about the broken cooling element in a cold cube.

She was safe. Now she waited. Whereas darkness had covered her entry, she would now use daylight as she proceeded. She had picked a highly traveled area of the compound for her path to approach the main building. She hoped that an officer in a patrol suit—they had no way of telling she was a cadet—would not be out of place here.

When the light through the vents of the toilet had grown bright enough, she stepped out. The canteen was closed, but she walked around it casually, even stopping when she reached the tables on the porch out front and searching the ground as if she had dropped something there the night before. A guard rounded the corner, patrolling the fence. After one look, he returned his attention to the perimeter.

Her first test passed, she walked with increased confidence towards the main building. A flip of her visor told her there was a great deal of movement inside. *All the better to be lost in,* she thought. Without hesitating, she waved Durp's security pass before the sensor. The door clicked and she entered.

The air on the other side was cold. A long hallway stretched out in front of her with white walls and a polished blue floor. The walls were set far apart, as if to accommodate large numbers of prisoners. Black glassy spheres set at intervals along the ceilings encased what she knew were security cameras. Doors on either side were also wide enough for a hospital bed to be rolled through. Spaced every few feet were alarm levers and speakers. Even more numerous were the locks set in the walls where a prisoner's chains could be secured.

For a moment, she worried that she was too early. The hallway was empty, but she started down its length anyway, aware that her safety depended upon her looking as if she belonged. An orderly in white passed through the T-junction at the end of the hall then disappeared from view. When two more passed, her hand floated to the empty sheath on her belt for her palm screen. She had left it with the cycle, but she wished she had it to bury her nose in now. The orderlies did not take much notice of her anyway.

The patrol suit bought her passage, but wandering the halls was not telling her much and it was only a matter of time before someone noticed her walking in circles. She decided to speak to the next person she saw. The opportunity came almost too soon. A man, not much older than she, emerged from a door on her right. He was tall and thin, his narrow wrists bearing a resemblance to the pens and styluses clicking loosely in the pocket of his lab coat. He wore a loose fitting shirt and casual shoes with no socks, an outfit that Sabrina would have expected to see on someone down at the wharves on sixth day. His beard was too thin to shave daily, but he had patchy fuzz on his chin and jaw. He stepped out of the door in a jaunty, relaxed manner, coming to a full stop when he saw her, his shoes making small, squeaking noises against the highly polished floor. His eyes traveled up and down the length of her suit.

"Can you help me?" Sabrina said with the same authoritative tone she would use on street patrol. "I'm supposed to have a tour of this place from Dr. Horwitz."

The young man pulled at the corners of his mouth. "Dr. Horwitz is usually not in for another hour."

"Well then, why'd Alex Durp tell me to come now?" She feigned growing anger. "Probably his idea of being funny."

"You report to Durp?"

"Yes. I'm Officer Xandes Phale," she said, taking the leap. Her status as a cadet could be taken away for that alone. "I'm filling in for him while he is on medical leave."

"I've seen your name on a lot of forms." The man extended his hand. "I can show you around. I'm Dr. Laurence Tripper, but you can call me Trip. Everyone here does."

"I need to be out of here and on my way back to Fortinbras in thirty minutes, Trip," Sabrina said, refusing his hand and instead checking the time on her visor, dispensing with common courtesies as she imagined Xandes might.

"Then let's get moving," he said, ignoring the slight. He opened the door he had just exited. "After you."

Sabrina stepped into a room with rows of examination tables, each fitted with restrains for a patient's arms, legs, and head. At the head of each table, a hinged arm held a helmet, the inside bristling with electrodes. A half dozen young workers were prepping syringes, filling them from bottles of fluid and setting them on metal trays beside the tables.

Trip introduced her to the others, sharing their names and how long they had been working there. Sabrina cut him off. "I'm not interested in every orderly's work history. What happens on the tables?"

"Well," Trip said, his mouth twisting downward for a moment. "This is where the initial treatment takes place." He casually flipped one of the thick belts. "The restraints are for the patient's own protection. They are injected with the necessary serums. It is standard to wait about an hour to let the drugs take their full effect and cross the blood-brain barrier. One of the side effects is increased anxiety, so patients are also injected with a sedative to calm them."

"They must not be too sedated if they need the restraints."

"Well, we find too much sedation dulls the effects of the other compounds. We have to strike the right balance for the most effective treatment."

"What is that hole for?" she asked of the drain at the center of each table.

Trip shifted from one foot to another and tugged at the corners of his mouth again, "Well, many patients are still nervous during the procedure. It's not uncommon for one or two to lose control of their bladders."

Trip's hand tapped the table soundlessly. Sabrina noticed the other staff glancing at her as they filled syringes.

"What exactly does the machine do to them?" she asked.

"It's the best possible solution to a challenging dilemma," Trip said, smiling. "Our wise Founders have decreed that no subject is to be harmed. Yet what do we do with a repeat offender or even a scrit whose mind is already too far gone to ever recover, but still too dangerous to himself and society to be released? The answer is this machine."

"The question was 'What does it do?'" Sabrina repeated.

Trip smiled. "It reduces neural density in the isocortex."

"You seem to have a talent for saying a lot but saying nothing, doctor," she said channeling Xandes' sour personality as best she could. "How about an explanation for someone who captures criminals and does not treat them?"

"We wipe the memories clean."

Sabrina fought the urge to swallow. "So they don't remember being a member of a cult and they can just return to normal life?"

"Well, not exactly. Let me take you outside and introduce you to some of our residents who have undergone treatment."

He led her out of the processing room, and they entered a long hallway with identical doors on either side. Each door had a window, and Trip urged her to look through one. On the other side were rows and rows of three-tiered bunk beds, each with identical white sheets spread over sleeping bodies. Farther down the hallway, two guards led a line of residents out of a similar room. None were restrained. Each was dressed in identical sky blue coveralls and cream undershirts. Men and women both had shaved heads.

"See, there is no banging here," Trip said. "No screaming. No terror. It is nothing like the detention wing at the station." He led her down the hallway, stopping them short of the row of residents marching out of the dormitory. They moved in an orderly line, each following in lockstep with the one in front. Their faces were placid, benign even, but hauntingly blank. The guards were relaxed, their sedation sticks stowed on their belts. When the last resident exited, Trip and Sabrina followed them through a door leading outside.

She blinked hard against the sunlight. Trip's own features folded and creased as he grimaced in the glare. The residents, moving in a straight line through a large field planted with legumes, did not seem to take notice of the sun. They walked quickly beyond the freshly sprouting plants to an empty plot where two more orderlies waited with a suspensor lift full of picks and shovels. The residents took tools, then moved to an open spot where they began mechanically turning the soil, preparing it for planting. Throughout the entire process, no one spoke. Only the picks and shovels made a sound. It was clockwork, each resident's motions as efficient and precise as a machine. Even the rows of soil they turned were perfectly straight and perfectly spaced.

"Memories are stored throughout the brain. So we can't selectively remove them," Trip said walking along a row of legumes. "Even if we could, who is to say they could return to their old life after being discovered as an occultist? Or in the case of a scrit, they are usually so damaged we can't find out where they are from. They don't know and we have no idea how they end up the way they do."

"I thought prisoners and scrits were rehabilitated."

"They are, but they are not returned to normal life," Trip said. "It's a common misperception. This is the best we can do for them." He moved beside a female, bent to read the number printed on her back and said, "6135, stop."

The woman ceased shoveling and stood at attention, her shovel in hand and her eyes staring straight into the distance. She was older than Sabrina, with elegant features and delicate smile lines beside the corners of her mouth. Sabrina imagined her to be a schoolteacher, for some reason, standing before a classroom of young students, the inspiration for more than a few school boy crushes. On a street in the city, with a full head of hair, she would have been striking.

Trip snapped his fingers before her face. Her eyes did not move. "See?" he said. "Reducing neural density in the isocortex blanks out their memories, their abstract thought, and along with it curiosity, superstition, rebellion."

"Their identities."

"Well, yes. That is their punishment. For scrits, it's not as if they had any in the first place. They are reduced to living through the brainstems. We've increased our precision enough to preserve basic functions like using a toilet, washing, and eating with utensils. Working keeps them active and healthy and supplies us with more than enough food. The surplus is sent to markets in the city."

"Is the process reversible?" Sabrina said. Her throat was dry, and her head felt light. She worked her heel into a mound of dirt in an effort to steady herself.

"Oh no, we're safe. They are not going to wake up any time soon. But look at this," he said as he called over to a male resident, who dropped his pick and marched over, as obedient as a pet dog. Trip arranged the male and female so that they were facing one another. He placed their hands in opposite positions on their shoulders and hips, then in the middle of the field he started singing a wordless melody, slapping out a rhythm on his thigh. Immediately, with robotic precision, the two residents began to dance, stepping and turning in careful unison, kicking up a cloud of dust at their feet. Trip flashed Sabrina a smile that was half bashful, half boastful. "One of our pastimes here is to see what we can teach them still, to see what skills can be established. This dance was my idea." He started clapping, turning his back to her as he followed the residents while keeping his commentary running. "I had to keep it simple, though. There is not too much left upstairs to work with."

Sabrina looked away. Each one of Trip's claps had felt like a blow to her head. She clenched and relaxed her fists. She scanned the fields and orchards. They seemed to stretch to the horizon, each filling with residents, pouring from the buildings, marching out in obedient, efficient rows.

One resident's face and build suddenly stood out to her. "Jacob?" she said. She trampled fresh rows of tilled soil as she ran to his side. He lifted and dropped his pick in unbroken rhythm. The markings, even the healing wounds on his arms, were unmistakable.

Please remember me. Please tell me they haven't yet—

"Stop. Jacob. Stop," she said, touching his shoulder, trying to slow his relentless digging.

"5625, Stop," Trip said, breathless after catching up to her.

Jacob stopped. Sabrina stood before him. With her hand on his chest, she could feel his heart beating.

"Jacob, it's me, Sabrina."

Trip was staring at her open-mouthed. She knew she must have looked a hysterical mess, but at the moment, she did not care. She laughed aloud with relief when Jacob's eyes focused on her and he smiled, but the expression slowly melted away, as if he was unable to maintain concentration. In another second, he was as blank as the other residents. Sabrina pounded his chest as if to wake him, but there was no response.

"You know him?" Trip said. She felt his eyes studying her with a cold skeptical objectivity that reminded her of D'Ag.

"He—he seemed a particularly pathetic case. I brought him in from Hill 36. He sort of got to me, I guess. I wanted to know he was doing well." Even as she spoke, she knew she was losing credibility. Her hands were shaking on his chest so she swung them around her and clasped them behind her back. "He seemed to recognize me."

"Yes, interesting that," Trip said, moving in front of Jacob. Jacob's eyes focused on him and he smiled again, only to have it fade as it did for Sabrina. "It's a reflex. Sometimes artifacts from the previous personality emerge like that. We focus on a face, we squint, we grimace, or we smile. He sees a face, he smiles. He must have been a friendly guy. He'll need some further treatment to get rid of it."

Sabrina did not hear Trip as they walked back to the compound. Guilt, confusion, urgency roiled in her mind. She had to speak to D'Ag. He needed to know what was happening, immediately.

She made some comment about having to leave, turning down Trip's offer to introduce her to Dr. Horwitz. Every moment that passed now was one wasted. Cold air washed over them as they reentered the building. She was vaguely aware of Trip asking her when she would be taking over duties for Officer Durp, when two of the larger guards came around the corner striding towards them purposefully, their sedation sticks out. Trip seemed to take notice of their posture and looked confused.

"Gentlemen, may I help you?"

The one on the right asked Sabrina to come with them. He had an athletic build, his broad shoulders tapering down to a narrow waist. The one of the left was older, with narrow eyes, a scarred cruel face, and a large gut like Durp.

"She is from the detention facilities at the station," Trip said. "I've been showing her around."

"I'd be happy to come along," Sabrina said with her best attempt at friendliness. This put Trip at ease. "I was running behind this morning and did not sign in at the front."

"Oh, well that would explain it—" Trip began, but the two men had moved in close enough. Sabrina had already discretely activated the grips on her hands and feet. She was outnumbered, but with the suit—and surprise—she had a chance to escape. She waited the span of two heartbeats, noting the way the two men moved. The closest was fluid, moving like an athlete. The second man was stiffer, favoring his right leg as if he had a cramp or congenital weakness. She breathed deep to relax her muscles as she would before a boxing match, even as the adrenaline made her limbs feel light and her heart race. Another breath. Aware of her entire body, she tried to lower her shoulders, even smile, hoping that it would persuade the men to let their guard down. The athlete reached out with his empty hand, his palm open, gesturing for her to move down the hallway in the direction they came from. The second man abruptly moved to the side, colliding with Trip. The athlete's eyes darted at them.

It was the break she wanted. Sabrina ran left and walked the wall, her boots gaining purchase even on the smooth polished surface. She took advantage of their surprise, running up the wall, planting herself then twisting to kick the back of the athlete's head.

He dropped with a thud that shook the floor. Sabrina landed and immediately ducked the swing of the other's sedation stick. The grips on her gloves snagged his pants, and she swept his leg, then she used the momentum to spin up while he fell down. Their places reversed, his head was bouncing off the floor when she smashed his face with her fist.

Two more guards sprinted around the corner.

No element of surprise this time.

She was not going to take them both on at once. She fired her grapple at one's ankle. Winches in her shoulder and elbow spun as the man slid across the floor to her feet. She leaped him, landing a kick in his face. The fourth guard rushed her, but his sedation stick was leading out too far. She kicked the tip, caught its handle, and let the guard's own motion carry him into the charged end. A yellow stain spread on his white pants before he collapsed with the others.

Trip was reaching for the emergency signal on the wall, but Sabrina's blaster was already trained on him.

"It's not on stun."

"You're not Officer Phale, are you?"

"What's in there?" she said, darting her eyes the nearest door.

"T-Textiles room. There will be residents … sewing."

"That one?"

"Empty. Storage."

"Open it, drag them in."

Trip obeyed, struggling with the weight of the men. When he had dragged in two, she picked up the others, her suit providing additional strength, and tossed them. Blood and urine remained smeared across the floor. She wiped it up quickly with one of the guards' jackets. The storage room was filled with the reassuring scents of sterile medical gauze and adhesive tape. She threw a box of tape at Trip's feet and told him to gag the guards. He was nothing if not obedient, wrapping their mouths thoroughly in layer after layer of tape. She removed prisoner restraints from her belt for him to lock their wrists and ankles.

"Now you," she said, turning him, locking his hands, and feet, then ripping open a box of gauze. Her vision flashed red with each beat of her heart.

"Just wait until D'Ag hears about all this," she said unrolling tape.

Trip turned his head, bewildered. "D'Ag hear about this? But D'Ag trained us. He built this. He built everything."

Chapter 14
Grapple

Sabrina had pushed the cycle too hard. The polycarbon cover of the last battery was melting, the viscous liquid dripping through the frame of the cycle onto the street below. The drips traced Sabrina's path through Fortinbras: down closed streets, over construction barriers, against the legal flow of traffic. When the power finally died and the steering column of the cycle locked, Sabrina coasted down a hill until she reached the intersection of Bakunin and Avalos where she leaped off, leaving the cycle to wobble into traffic. She was already halfway down the block when she heard a CRP crash into her riderless cycle. She didn't look back. The afternoon jams were just beginning. People were clogging the sidewalks, so she kept to the street where a pedal cyclist's shoulder hit her face as she collided with him, her momentum turning him end-over-end.

She got up and kept running. She knew she ought to have a plan, but she could not think past simply getting Lindsey out of her cell and away from … everything and everyone. Each person she passed on the street seemed to her either a spy or an occultist. The very buildings loomed forward to trap her. Whom could she trust now? With every corner she rounded, she clenched her teeth with the fear of seeing a second prisoner transport, this one with Lindsey on it. She kept trying to force her mind to think ahead, just as she had done along every rise and every bend as she had raced back through the desert, but her thoughts kept returning to three facts:

She had captured Lindsey. She had put her best friend in danger. D'Ag knew everything.

All afternoon she had tried to invent possibilities where all the pieces fit together. Perhaps D'Ag had built the compound and trained the scientists, but an overly enthusiastic administrator—Dr. Horwitz—had turned the place into the nightmare it was now. As hard as she tried to convince herself, the thought that D'Ag would let anything escape his attention just did not sit with her.

He knew. He has always known.

The vehicle bay was busy. This time of afternoon, the station was at its fullest as officers on the day shift parked their cruisers and cycles in charging ports, and their replacement officers dressed and prepped. Sabrina wiped her hair from her face as she crossed the bay and slowed as much as her anxiety would allow. Detention crews in their white padded uniforms were loading a transport at the far end of the bay. Lindsey was not among them. Despite her haste, the expressions on the prisoner's faces stuck in her mind: resignation, fear, loss.

They knew. They knew and Lindsey had known. Sabrina had been the ignorant one all this time.

And D'Ag had kept her that way.

The doors to the detention wing parted. Xandes sat behind the counter. Sabrina double-checked the cells with her visor. The infrared revealed figures behind her, each curled into similar frightened shapes. One of them was Lindsey.

She flipped up the visor. Xandes' smiling visage awaited her.

"Cadet Sabryia, how are you? That was some trick you played—"

She stopped when Sabrina raised her blaster to her face. She looked for some sense of cold determination within herself, but found none. The tremors in her hand were causing her weapon to shake. She was surprised at Xandes' calm and how she simply stared blankly at Sabrina and the gun that was pointed at her.

"You know what this is?" Sabrina finally said.

"I do," Xandes replied, standing up slowly, spreading her hands on the counter top, the artery in her neck throbbing. "But I want to give you a moment to reconsider."

"You don't know what they do to them."

"I do know what it is like to be a woman here, Sabrina. You do this, we'll always be seen as soft."

Sabrina had not expected this. For her part, Xandes kept her hands still and her body straight. Only her eyes moved, glancing at the video screens behind her desk. "You have changed things for us. A week ago, I had given up the idea of being on patrol. Now it's a possibility. Don't ruin it. Don't ruin it for all of us. You can still put it away."

Sabrina thumbed the blaster's discharge to a higher setting, a show of bravado that she didn't possess.

Something in Xandes' face slammed shut. Her movements became swift and efficient as she led Sabrina to the detention block, her hands out to her sides in full view, a perfect study in the obedient prisoner. Sweat was pouring down Sabrina's sides and dripping off her forehead. She waited a safe distance behind while Xandes punched a code into a keypad that opened the door to the corridor where Lindsey was housed. Her cell was nearly at the end of the hall. Sabrina was aware with each step of the greater distance they would need to cover in their escape. The scrits screamed and pounded. This time, Xandes made no outraged cry for silence. When they finally reached Lindsey's cell, she did not hesitate to swipe her card and step inside. She crossed to the far corner and held up her hands.

Sabrina followed her in slowly. But for a toilet anchored to the wall and a sink, the room was bare and empty. Opposite them was a sleeping mat where a figure lay trembling beneath a sheet. Lindsey's bells tinkled as she shook. Sabrina knelt down, placing her hand on her shoulder and calling Lindsey's name. When she did not respond, Sabrina rolled her onto her back and said her name again. Lindsey lifted her head opened her eyes then lost focus, her eyes rolling up in their sockets.

Please don't be like Jacob.

Sabrina swung her blaster back at Xandes. "What did you do to her?"

"She suffers from visual and auditory hallucinations. We adjusted her medication. It is a common treatment for those with her condition."

"Adjusted?"

"Twenty times the normal dosage. It usually results in an increase of symptoms for about 24 hours, but when they subside the patient is normally completely cured."

She turned to Lindsey, shaking her, "Lindsey! Lindsey! Can you hear me?"

"Sabrina," Lindsey said, her speech slurred. Her hands tightened around Sabrina's arms. "I knew you were coming."

"We're going."

"She has a blaster."

Sabrina snapped her head around to see Xandes standing with her legs apart, a blaster in her hands.

"Xandes, if you saw what they did …" Sabrina said.

"I don't care," Xandes said. "I gave you your chance. Now face the wall."

Sabrina's blaster was still in her hand, but she had lowered it when she had checked on Lindsey. Xandes had her. She repeated her command. Sabrina was turning to the wall when Lindsey began to speak. It was her distant voice, a whisper, the same voice she used when speaking from that place where her visions came.

"You snapped the kittens' necks by a sewer, then dropped them in," she said, the sibilant words echoing off the bare walls. "The first one went straight in, but the second, it dropped by the lip and rolled. I can see it too, through your eyes. That stayed with you the longest, how its body, the fur, soft, cushioning it so it barely made a sound, its body turning so loosely and relaxed down into nothingness. It was such a contrast to when they were alive, when they were alive and moved."

The whites in Xandes' eyes had grown large, and her body was as rigid as stone. Lindsey's eyes blinked rapidly as she fought to remain lucid. Her hands trembled as she clutched the edges of Sabrina's suit.

"Xandes," Lindsey said, "Your parents gave you and your sister the kittens. Then your sister got sick and died, and you could not understand how they could have lived—pets, *animals*—and your sister die. So you killed them both. Told your parents they had run away."

The barrel of the gun moved, and something strange began to happen to Xandes' face. It started with a deepening of the creases at the corner of her mouth then spread to her neck, where her tendons corded. The muscles on her jaw bunched, and she shook her head back and forth. "Nobody knew. Nobody could know." Her head nodded forward as if her breath had stopped. Finally, she shut her eyes and was wracked by sobs. Her blaster clattered to the floor as she wrapped her arms around herself and dropped to her knees.

"I was the pretty one," she coughed. "She was the tough one." She doubled over and touched her forehead to the floor. Sabrina swiped up her weapon and turned to grab Lindsey. Xandes crawled across the room, her hands slapping the bare floor before she grabbed Lindsey's gown in her fists. "Tell me. Tell me she is in a better place, please."

Lindsey did not respond. Upon standing, she had lost consciousness again, falling into Sabrina's arms. Sabrina struggled with her weight with one arm while fending Xandes off with the other. She pried the prison guard's fingers loose, no longer able to bring herself to shoot her, even with a stun.

In the corridor, Sabrina could barely hear the screams and moans of the other prisoners over the rush of blood in her ears. Lindsey woke and made token motions with her legs, as if walking, but that only slowed them further. Halfway down the hall, Sabrina threw her over her shoulder and began to run, stopping when they reached the door at the end of the corridor. It was locked. Sabrina tried Durp's pass, but it had been deactivated.

Sabrina was lifting her blaster to the key pad when Lindsey's eyes snapped open, "Four, two, five, eight, nine, six, seven, seven, one."

Sabrina punched the code in and a green light flashed just before the door slid open. "How did you know?"

"I just see, see everything. I looked at the key pad, and I could see all the times those numbers had been punched. I could see all the people brought through the door. I can see them when they come here looking for us in a few minutes. I can't make it stop."

Sabrina carried Lindsey past the admissions desk and towards the hall that led to the vehicle bay, her weapon drawn. Lindsey hissed, "Left, left, through that door."

"That is not the way to the—"

"Do it. They're coming!"

Sabrina pushed opened the door to a storage closet. Footsteps sounded behind them. She flung Lindsey in ahead of her and swung the door closed, leaving it open just a crack behind them. Two officers passed. As Sabrina pushed open the door again, Lindsey shuddered and whispered, "Wait, one more."

On cue, a third officer ran past.

"It's all right. Go," Lindsey said from the back of the closet.

"You can see them coming?"

"Yes. Hurry."

Lindsey turned them down two more hallways. They were not the turns Sabrina would have taken to the vehicle bay, but each time they narrowly avoided officers or detention guards. While they waited in a hallway for a delivery boy to turn a corner, Lindsey mumbled, "They know."

"They know what?"

"That you betrayed them."

A siren pierced the air above them, sounding throughout the building, announcing a detention breach. A voice crackled in Sabrina's earpiece announcing that Cadet Sabryia had just assaulted an officer and was trying to escape with a prisoner. Then it went dead. They had cut her off from the network.

"Crite," Sabrina said, remembering what they did to criminals who assault officers and wondering how much worse it would be for a cadet.

"Turn now."

"What?"

"Turn now, right."

Sabrina obeyed, pulling them down a narrow corridor lined with windowless offices, each closed and locked. It was a hallway she had never seen before and one she never would have taken. Sabrina hefted her up to her shoulder. Lindsey's muscles still had a relaxed, rubbery quality to them. They proceeded on a circuitous route through the station, each turn allowing them to elude officers on their way to the detention wing.

The end of the hall opened into a wing of the station under construction. They passed between piles of building materials, idle construction machinery, and through curtains of plastic sheeting. Footsteps pounded the floor above and below, but the hallway on this floor was empty.

"Down the stairs, fast!" Lindsey said.

Sabrina kicked open a door to a nearby stairwell, her feet flying from one step to the other as she descended onto a floor that smelled of fresh paint.

"Through the door, shoot from left to right."

Sabrina opened door with her shoulder and charged through, weapon raised. She was in one of the new teaching wings on the station. Classrooms lined the corridor. Three figures came running around the corner simultaneously. Pitt, Boyle, and Abner halted upon seeing her, bumping into the other. Abner, on the left, had his own weapon raised to his shoulder, like a good cadet. Sabrina stunned him first, then Boyle, who was quick enough to draw his blaster but not quick enough to aim it. Pitt knew better than to waste time arming himself. He stepped to his left, avoiding Sabrina's blast then closed in with two quick steps. His left hand swept downward to his belt powering up his suit while his right struck Sabrina's blaster hard enough to send it across the floor. He leaned back and kicked her, his heavy boot knocking her against the wall. Lindsey slipped from her shoulder with a cry.

Sabrina raised her fists. She had beaten instructors in the ring, and with her suit on she had added speed, power, and protection. She was as confident boxing as she was shooting. But Pitt knew this, too. She punched twice. He blocked one with his forearm, the other landed on his side, but his suit protected him. He lowered his shoulder and drove her against the wall.

Spots danced in front of her eyes as she realized her miscalculation: as one of the grappling instructors, Pitt knew her strengths and weaknesses. She was at a disadvantage grappling where size mattered. He had just shifted the advantage to himself.

She struck downward at his collarbones, but she might as well have been hitting sandbags. She swung for his head. He ducked and while low to the ground his hand clamped around her ankle. The next moment the room was spinning as he swung her upside down. He pitched her into the wall. His suit augmented his strength, just as Sabrina's protected her, absorbing some of the impact as the bricks shattered beneath her. Her legs and arms felt heavy and stiff as she tried to get up. Pitt was on her again, tossing her up into the ceiling.

The hall went dark as the lights shattered. Glass and wiring dropped to the floor. Sabrina had barely made it to her elbows before Pitt grabbed her shoulders, swung her in a tight circle, and released her. Time slowed as she flailed, suspended in the air, before she crashed through a glass window and tumbled across the rows of seating in an unopened classroom.

Pain suffused her body. She could not see Lindsey now as she struggled to extricate herself from the desks and chairs that still smelled of new fabric and paint. Pitt had flung her through one of the observation windows where instructors could monitor students while taking exams. Now he was kicking at the locked door. Sabrina scrambled for the window, but her head was spinning, her movements clumsy and uncoordinated. The door burst open. Pitt stretched out and caught her by the leg. She spun and swung for his face, but she was too slow. He grabbed her by her belt and flung her down on a desk. He did not leave time for her to recover. He yanked her up and slammed her onto to the desk again. Her shoulders and back felt as if they would splinter to pieces. Pitt lifted her above his head once more and drove her for a third time into the desktop. This time it cracked and collapsed.

Sabrina tasted blood in her mouth as she tried to rise. Pitt curled an arm around her hips and threw her end-over-end into the corner of the room. She lay where she had slid down the wall, a shard of the desk she had managed to grab brandished in her hand. When Pitt came in again she stabbed him, but the wood simply splintered against the mesh of his suit. He grabbed her neck now, the adhesive grips of his gloves activating and tearing at her skin. Her feet were off the ground, and he began to clamp down with irresistible pressure.

Spit gathered on his lips as he spoke through clenched teeth, "Now, you learn your place."

Sabrina's breath wheezed in her throat. The room darkened. Her swipes at Pitt were useless. She had one option left. She aimed her grapple at the exposed flesh of Pitt's neck, but he anticipated her and struck her wrist. The grapple fired wide, the line whizzing over his shoulder. A smile crept into the corner of his mouth. "Would have killed me, shooting that into me. That's all the justification I need."

The pressure around her neck increased. Her sight was failing her, but something punched through the growing hood of unconsciousness: a sensation in her fingertips as electrodes in the derm links of her gloves relayed messages through her nerve endings to her brain: her grapple had locked onto something.

Her last thought before oblivion took her was simply *retract*. In the new suit, a mere thought was enough. Her arm pulled straight. The winches sprung to life and dragged some object across the floor with a loud screech. A desk slammed into the back of Pitt's knees, dropping him against its top. He released Sabrina. She gasped, snapping off one of the desk legs as she hit the floor. The broken desk tipped, dumping Pitt. He sprung up, just in time for Sabrina to connect.

The first strike stunned him, snapping his head sideways. As he wobbled, Sabrina wound up and swung again. This time the desk leg broke off in her hand and pieces struck the wall along with a string of Pitt's blood. He fell with a heavy thud alongside the wreckage of the destroyed classroom. Only a few inches of the leg remained. She threw the piece on Pitt's motionless body and limped outside through the door Pitt had shattered. Boyle and Abner were still unconscious, left where she had stunned them. Lindsey was slumped against the wall, like a paraplegic dumped from her wheelchair.

"Sabrina, you're bleeding," she said as Sabrina helped her up.

"Not as bad as Pitt. Let's go."

Chapter 15
Annaliese

Boyle and Abner were unconscious but still alive. Sabrina ripped off Boyle's headset and visor and put them on. She could hear the chatter of officers searching the floors of the station. Superimposed on her vision was a map of the station, the secured wings glowing blue. She quickly punched in a message that their wing was locked down. She knew the station security would try to track her own headset so she removed its power source. She could use Boyle's now, and she took Abner's for good measure.

Lindsey's directions had served them well. They were adjacent to the vehicle bay, and an unfinished wall allowed them to slip through to a charging cruiser. The batteries would be low, but the methaline tanks were full. Sabrina belted Lindsey in as her eyes rolled back again.

"Come on, stay with me, Lindsey."

"Sabrina, I see darkness, full of light. Broken pieces of light and stone."

Sabrina ducked behind the fender as two cadets ran past. Once they were gone, she unhitched the cruiser from the charging post and climbed into the driver's seat. She rolled down the rows of parked vehicles slowly, as any cruiser on its way out to patrol would do. With all the commotion there was no one watching the ramp as Sabrina pulled the vehicle up and entered the flow of traffic. She waited until they turned the corner off Avalos Street before she stopped, replaced the power source in her own headset, got out, and tossed it into the back of a passing vegetable lorry. She gave Abner's to a boy on a pedal cycle, telling him he could only have it if he rode away from her as fast as he could. He disappeared around the corner, his legs pumping madly. She got back in, slammed her foot down on the pedal, and started the siren wailing. It was not long before she passed other cruisers speeding in the opposite direction, responding to urgent calls back at the station. She felt protected by the mirrored windows, but she knew it was not long before they figured out her trick.

Lindsey grabbed her arm. Tears were running down her face, "I'm sorry. I never knew."

"Never knew what?"

"After you beat up Sylvia at school, they made you clean the toilets for a month at recess. They didn't even give you gloves."

Sabrina smiled for the first time that day. "I never wanted you to know. I did not want you to feel guilty. I'd do it again, for you."

Lindsey held her hand until she passed out again. Sabrina put Lindsey's hand in her lap and put both hands back on the wheel. She swung the vehicle around onto Mill Street, dodging and weaving around pedestrians in crosswalks. Once she passed through Quine Circle and was on the Bay Road, she yanked the power lever, shifting propulsion from the cruiser's batteries to the methaline turbines. The engines roared to life, and she and Lindsey were thrown against their seats. Long and wedge-shaped, the cruisers were built to be the fastest vehicles on the road. CRPs flew past as if they were stationary.

But Sabrina did not know where she was driving. Her only thought had been to escape the city. Now where would they go? The Head Ministry, where D'Ag waited? Never. North was impossible, the lands beyond Lysander were uninhabitable with radiation. She knew there were empty lands to the south between the edges of the city and the wall, but what chance would the two of them stand in the wilderness?

Voices in her ear had determined that the locating beacon from her headset in the vegetable lorry was a decoy. The same with Abner's. Time was running out. She watched the fuel and temperature gauges on the instrument panel of the cruiser. Their speed was slowly charging the batteries. When she lifted the lid on the supply box at their feet, she saw it was full. Each cruiser had at least three days of food and water as well as thermal blankets.

Three days and then what?

"There were people here once," Lindsey said, pressing her hand to the window, brown lands running past her fingers.

"What people?"

"People sent away. Then others came. They all called it home. They had lost so much. It was so sad. So much pain."

Sabrina rubbed the wheel with her thumb, wondering how strong a dose they had given Lindsey. She pictured Jacob and his flat, dead-eyed stare. Her thumbnail peeled off a piece of the steering wheel grip as Lindsey began to drift away again.

"Lindsey. Lindsey, stay with me."

The turn to the Head Ministry approached on their left and disappeared. They were rolling down a road Sabrina had traveled with her uncle only a few times, when he had taken her with him to visit orchards and fields managed by the ministry. Wind blew in from the sea and sent curtains of sand across their path and over the cruiser in long, curling eddies.

A black shape metastasized outside Sabrina's window. A shape that screamed like a child. A barrage of green light flooded the cockpit of the car.

A L'ved.

A white number 3 stood out against the black exoskeleton. The L'ved's turbines were whining at full blast, twin cones of blue flame rippling, the ailerons tipping and turning with small adjustments as the machine tried to identify her and Lindsey. Sabrina slapped down her visor before the beams traced her face, buying her a few moments to power down the window. The heat of the desert and the L'ved engines poured over her like a furnace. She suppressed a cough in her throat. Her skin was suddenly flush with sweat. The noise and heat woke Lindsey, her eyes growing wide at the sight of the machine so close. The L'ved rocked in the vortexes thrown off by the cruiser, the plating and limbs rearranging as it sought a more aerodynamic configuration. The chrome struts that connected the turbines to the body gleamed as they extended, one segment telescoping to another. Sabrina depressed the blaster setting to its most lethal, took aim out the window, and fired.

A blue arc danced and dissipated as currents shorted out in the machine. The stabilizing surfaces of the wings froze, and the L'ved's body tipped downward, dragging along the road. A rooster tail of sparks erupted and road fragments pinged at the side of the vehicle. The starboard thruster choked in a gush of exhaust. The pitch of the remaining engine crescendoed as the L'ved compensated for the sudden loss of power and leveled out.

"Hold on," Sabrina said. She yanked the wheel and slammed the cruiser into the L'ved. The vehicle rocked as warnings and alarms screamed. Lindsey braced herself against the dashboard as Sabrina righted the wheel and the L'ved tumbled alongside like a cannon ball. After bouncing a few more times, it rolled off to the shoulder in a cloud of dust and smoke.

Sabrina tried to see the machine in the side view mirror, but it had been sheared off in the collision.

"Where did it go?"

"Behind us," Lindsey said. The noise of the thruster at full blast closed in on them. The cruiser lurched forward, the bottom scraping the road.

"It's trying to tear off our thruster," Sabrina said. She struggled against the forces in the wheel as the L'ved tore the covers of the engines away. Her blaster on its highest setting, she fired a volley of shots out the back, blowing out the window. The shaking of the wheel brought her attention back to the road. She had strayed onto the shoulder, and a sign smacked against the windscreen and tumbled over them before she pulled back onto the road. The L'ved closed in on the cruiser's thrusters again, one of its limbs converted into a grasping claw. A warning on the dash indicated that pressure in the propulsion system was dropping. One of the injection cylinders was already off line. Straightening the vehicle, Sabrina checked Lindsey's seatbelt, then her own, before standing on the brake pedal.

They were flung against their belts as the inside of the cruiser exploded with the impact of the L'ved, striking against the frame behind, then again on the nose of the cruiser, as it tumbled end-over-end. It was in front of them, rolling, a mess of flashing sunlight and creaking metal. A drunken man. The machine tried to arrest its momentum, dropping an arm that had morphed into a grapple.

"No, you don't," Sabrina said. She punched the accelerator training the center of the cruiser on the machine as it struggled to stand upright.

"Duck! Blade!" Lindsey pulled Sabrina down across the seats. Another crash. Another thumping against the roof of the vehicle. This time when Sabrina sat up, the wind blew through her hair. When she leaned back she found that the top of her seat had been shorn away along with the top of the windscreen and the rear view mirror. She turned in her seat to see the number three L'ved attempting to stand up again. The top of the cruiser lay on the road like the top of a tin can. The L'ved was listing to one side, but the limb reshaped into a long sword-like blade was unmistakable.

"I guess I made him angry," Sabrina said, righting the wheel before the cruiser rolled off the road. She thought she had seen flashing blue lights on the road behind the L'ved, but before she could turn and look again, Lindsey was screaming.

"Another, from the sky."

A second L'ved was descending onto the road, thrusters burning bright blue.

Prey. Running out of options.

The number on its shoulder identified it as 5. It lifted an arm, and the air around it shimmered, like a mirage in sunlight. Sabrina recognized the edges of the expanding bubble moving towards them.

"Iza," she spat.

The sound pulse grew, invisible but for the edge where the powerful mix of high and low frequency waves blurred the light. It was a pure pulse of sound that would shatter anything inflexible—the cruiser— leaving them shaken to the point of sickness but physically intact. As intact as they could be when the cruiser disintegrated around them at top speed.

The bubble soon engulfed the entire road, distorting the image of the L'ved beyond to make Number 5 seem much smaller. Dust and particles from the road were gathering in a wave at the base. An access road was coming up on their left, and Sabrina swung the cruiser in that direction, turning them broadside to the wave. It struck the back half of the vehicle in a loud "whump" that knocked the air out of her chest. The turbines went tumbling into the hardpan, disintegrating into their component parts with each cartwheel. Battery power took over as Sabrina crashed them onto a dirt road, spinning the front tires and dragging what was left of the back of the cruiser along the ground.

The front of the cruiser was smoking as they powered up the road, the sound of sirens in pursuit behind them. A whole line of vehicles with flashing lights filled the road to the north. Number 5 was tracking them on the ground, following at a cautious pace. Number 3 was nowhere to be seen.

The road ended outside a tall, windowless building—an automated water processing facility. Sabrina spent the last dregs of power from the battery to pull them up as close to the front door as possible. Lindsey got out on her own accord, leaning on the cruiser frame for support, her eyes wide at the empty space where the back of the vehicle had been.

"You came here with D'Ag once," she said panting, her eyes blinking, as if trying to sort out the image she saw in her mind with the one presented by her eyes.

"Yes," Sabrina said, checking over her shoulder at Number 5 stalking through the brush towards them. "It was an inspection trip."

The weapons locker on the side of the vehicle had been damaged but not destroyed. She emptied it of its contents: a plasma rifle, sonic detonators, sedation sticks. She used the plasma rifle to blow open the door to the building. Before Number 5 came any closer, she grabbed a satchel of sonic detonators in one hand and Lindsey with the other. Once inside, Sabrina blocked the door by overturning a cart of spare pipes and valves. Over the clamor, she could just hear a voice calling out to her on a loud speaker from one of the vehicles pulling up outside.

Machinery hummed softly all around them. The air was heavy and warm with moisture.

"He is out there," Lindsey announced, leaning against a sweating pipe.

"Who?"

"Your uncle."

"Got any other ideas about how we get out of here?"

"No, but I know you once kissed Doug Nichlos."

"Had onion breath. I didn't tell you." Sabrina headed towards a set of metal stairs. "But that is not going to help us. Can't you dream up a scenario to take on a hundred officers?"

Lindsey shook her head. "It doesn't work that way. Things are just coming to me in flashes. It's like it's whoever or whatever is in front of me, I see their past, their future."

An animal instinct was driving Sabrina upward. She took Lindsey by the hand and led her up the staircase, which connected to a series of catwalks. They crossed cisterns of dark water. At every opportunity, Sabrina took them higher, the air warming and filling with the smell of steam, charcoal and sand. They both were breathing heavily from the climb, the gentle noise of humming machines and trickling water strangely soothing. As they caught their breath on a landing Lindsey stiffened. "The door! They are about to—"

A deafening sound drowned out the pumps and reverberated throughout the plant. The echoes faded and were replaced by the drumbeat and rattle of feet climbing the stairs.

"Come on!" Sabrina said, grabbing Lindsey's hand again.

Lindsey struggled, nearly losing her balance over a railing. Sabrina caught her. Officers sprinted across the plant's floor several stories below. She wrapped her arm around Lindsey again as an officer grappled and winched himself up to the end of the catwalk behind them.

She turned her blaster on him, but before she could fire, D'Ag's voice called out from below, "Don't shoot, hold your fire!"

The officer's blaster was trained on her, but his trigger finger did not move. Sabrina started up another set of stairs, the catwalks shaking now with the pounding of so many climbing feet. Grappling hooks lodged in the struts and joists of the catwalks and wound more officers upward. Another officer appeared a level below them, peering through a dark visor. She felt a disturbing sympathy for every scrit, occultist, and petty criminal she had ever chased down.

So this is how we look. Impervious. Cold.

Her uncle continued to beseech everyone to hold their fire. They all must have known her identity by now—her real identity, her secret revealed in her uncle's own wild pursuit, his strained pleas.

How they must have hated her. But if it kept them from firing, she would take advantage of it. She helped Lindsey up a last set of stairs that climbed between two fat, bulging cisterns and through a door to the roof. There was nowhere else to go.

She did not bother closing the latch behind them. It was no use, and Sabrina was too weary from carrying Lindsey. Her motions had to be simple and efficient now. The roof was covered with shimmering pools, water pumped up from below and undulating large patches of algae. They negotiated the narrow walks that formed a grid between the pools while officers poured out of the hatch, slowly cutting off one avenue of escape after another. Sabrina simply reacted now. She had no plan, except to move in the direction away from the officers.

Prey. Cornered.

The remaining catwalks led her to the far end of the building, where a large channel sluiced excess water from the pools down the side of the building and to an inlet where the sea churned between sheer cliffs. The sun, resting on the eastern horizon, turned the water a fire red.

A scream and a grinding noise tore the air as Number 5 circled overhead, then alighted, the talons curling around the metal skeleton of the building like a raptor. The walks were swarming with armed officers now, each identical in their patrol suits. Did she know any of them? She had to. The catwalks ended, and she stepped into the channel of running water that rose to her shins. Below the lip of the channel, she was out of sight of the officers. The water was warm from collecting in the sunlight. While they were hidden from sight, Sabrina dropped a sonic detonator charge into the flow, armed it, and held it against the current with her foot. As officers appeared at the end of the channel, she backed towards the edge with Lindsey in one arm and the detonator beneath her boot.

The L'ved circled and landed in a new position, gazing down at her through its impenetrable convex face.

Then D'Ag was there. By all appearances—the wrinkled slacks, the unbuttoned shirt damp with sweat—he had been ripped from his work by the unfolding situation. How she had humiliated him, their great leader, his personal life displayed so openly before his subjects, his complete lack of control, his disheveled state. Sabrina could not determine what she felt when she looked at him. It was better to see him than the weapons aimed at her, but at the same time all he represented to her was betrayal.

He splashed into the water. "Sabrina, please stop this."

"I've seen what they do, D'Ag." She raised her gun at him. "I've seen what they do. Tell me you didn't know."

He lifted his hands, palms outward, and shook his head, "Sabrina, I should have told you."

"How could you let it happen to her?" Sabrina said, wrapping her arm more tightly around Lindsey, continuing to back down the sluice of water as her uncle followed gingerly, slipping once to his knees, then righting himself. Officers dropped into the water behind him, fanning out into a line. Sabrina checked over her shoulder to make sure none were circling back behind her.

"Please, I can explain everything. It is my own fault I have not shared the entire truth with you," D'Ag pleaded, his face etched with worry.

Lindsey stiffened in Sabrina's arm and shook as another tremor took her. The spell did not last long, but when she came out of it Lindsey clung to Sabrina more tightly than before, her nails scratching against the mesh of Sabrina's suit. She looked back and forth between D'Ag and Sabrina, her eyes full of poison.

"How could you do that to her?" she said between her teeth, her arms tightening around Sabrina.

Something Sabrina had never seen appeared in D'Ag's face: fear. He stepped towards them, only to slip again in the water to his knees. He tried to steady himself, waving his arms, "Lindsey, don't—"

"He killed your parents, Sabrina!"

The water swirling at their feet seemed to grow stronger. A tern wailed and tipped against a landscape of red clouds. Water, thrown up by the disrupted current, gathered in gleaming drops like quicksilver on the beams of the building, beams where in places the paint had blistered beneath spreading scabs of rust. Lindsey steadied Sabrina now. They had reached the edge of the channel, and ocean waves crashed in an inlet far below them. The buzz of locusts rose from a grassy ledge below. Sabrina felt completely hollow, her insides scooped away, and what was left of her only a thin residue clinging to a dying, empty shell. She knew the only reason she could stand on those hollow columns that were once her legs was Lindsey, straining against the current to support her own dead weight.

D'Ag's hand was wrapped about his middle, as if he had been kicked, his lips pale and trembling. "Sabrina, there is so much you do not understand."

She used the hollow limb that used to be her arm to point the gun directly at her uncle's face.

"Tell me. The whole truth."

He kept to one knee but steadied himself with the other leg bent, reaching his hands out to her. "I'm so sorry. I'm so sorry. I had no choice."

She nearly shot him, but Lindsey stayed her, for whatever reason, placing her hand on her hollow forearm. Tears were blinding her now. The L'ved, the officers, the shining sun all working into a blur. She fought Lindsey, lifting the gun again. D'Ag was motionless, staring blankly at her, his mouth, his cheeks, his jaws sagging. She heard pleading sounds from Lindsey, but not the words. Her own voice came out in a whisper, the question driven by some seed of doubt placed there so long before, germinating only now.

"What is my real name, D'Ag?"

The answer seemed to come to mind as soon as the word left his lips, as if it was a puzzle piece she already knew by the shape of its absence.

"Annaliese."

The only sound was the water rushing past. Every weapon remained aimed in their direction. Sabrina lowered her own, but did not let go, lest the officers rush forward.

"D'Ag," she said, wrapping her free arm around Lindsey. Lindsey seemed to understand. She took hold of Sabrina's belt with both hands and pressed herself close. "Promise me something."

"Anything."

"Don't try to follow us."

Before he could answer, Sabrina lifted her foot off the sonic charge and threw herself and Lindsey over the edge. They fell in a curtain of suspended water before the whump of thunder exploded. The railings and skin of the treatment plant twisted free into the air, pliable as ribbon. Then the shockwave struck them, sending them down, faster, farther, arm and arm, into the waiting sea.

THANK YOU FOR READING

If you enjoyed volume one, all volumes are available wherever books are sold online. Please leave a review, they help us writers a lot.

"When I have a little money, I buy books; and if I have any left,
I buy food and clothes."
–Erasmus

Please consider supporting the Equal Justice Initiative at www.EJI.com